ARE ALL
GUYS
ASSHOLES?

ARE ALL GUYS ASSHOLES?

More Than 1,000 Guys in 10 Cities Reveal Why They're Not, Why They Sometimes Act Like They Are, and How Understanding Their Real Feelings Will Solve Your Guy Drama Once and for All

Amber Madison

JEREMY P. TARCHER/PENGUIN
a member of Penguin Group (USA) Inc.
New York

JEREMY P. TARCHER/PENGUIN
Published by the Penguin Group
Penguin Group (USA) Inc., 375 Hudson Street, New York, New York 10014, USA •
Penguin Group (Canada), 90 Eglinton Avenue East, Suite 700, Toronto, Ontario M4P 2Y3,
Canada (a division of Pearson Penguin Canada Inc.) • Penguin Books Ltd, 80 Strand,
London WC2R 0RL, England • Penguin Ireland, 25 St Stephen's Green, Dublin 2, Ireland
(a division of Penguin Books Ltd) • Penguin Group (Australia), 250 Camberwell Road,
Camberwell, Victoria 3124, Australia (a division of Pearson Australia Group Pty Ltd) •
Penguin Books India Pvt Ltd, 11 Community Centre, Panchsheel Park, New Delhi–110 017,
India • Penguin Group (NZ), 67 Apollo Drive, Rosedale, North Shore 0632, New Zealand
(a division of Pearson New Zealand Ltd) • Penguin Books (South Africa) (Pty) Ltd,
24 Sturdee Avenue, Rosebank, Johannesburg 2196, South Africa

Penguin Books Ltd, Registered Offices: 80 Strand, London WC2R 0RL, England

Most Tarcher/Penguin books are available at special quantity discounts for bulk purchase for
sales promotions, premiums, fund-raising, and educational needs. Special books or book excerpts
also can be created to fit specific needs. For details, write Penguin Group (USA) Inc.
Special Markets, 375 Hudson Street, New York, NY 10014.

Library of Congress Cataloging-in-Publication Data

Madison, Amber.
Are all guys assholes? : more than 1,000 guys in 10 cities reveal why they're not,
why they sometimes act like they are, and how understanding their real
feelings will solve your guy drama once and for all / Amber Madison.
p.   cm.
ISBN 978-1-58542-880-9
1. Man-woman relationships—Psychological aspects.   2. Men—Psychology.
3. Dating (Social customs)—Psychological aspects.   I. Title.
HQ801.M333   2011   2011027802
306.73—dc23

Printed in the United States of America
1   3   5   7   9   10   8   6   4   2

BOOK DESIGN BY MEIGHAN CAVANAUGH

To all the wonderful men in my life,

who restore my faith daily

CONTENTS

When I Screwed Him Last Night, Did I Also Screw Our Shot at a Relationship?
SEX AND DATING

Does He Not Care Like I Do?
GUYS AND RELATIONSHIPS

Is His Sexuality More Complex Than "Pork It"?
GUYS AND SEX *170*

Good Thinking, Asshole!
SEEMINGLY ASSHOLE MINDSETS WE
SHOULD ADOPT FOR OURSELVES *192*

Kissing Assholes Good-bye
HOW TO IDENTIFY ONE, BREAK FREE,
OR GET ONE TO CHANGE HIS TUNE *213*

How I Became
an Asshololologist

Leave it to two baggy-jeans-wearing, diamond-stud-rocking, 40-in-paper-bag-sipping dudes to change your thoughts on guys forever. I was two weeks into my man journey and thoroughly convinced it was the worst idea I'd ever had. Then, on this beautiful San Francisco Sunday, as the symphony played at Dolores Park, two thugged-out-looking 20-somethings asked me for advice.

Guy: "Okay, I told you my thoughts on girls. Now I want your help."

"All right." Suspecting I was getting into it for the long haul, I took a seat.

Guy: "So I kinda like this girl . . ."

Friend: "Kinda like? Come on, bro, you're obsessed with her."

Guy: "*Fine.* I really like this girl. Last night, I take her out, it's goin' well, and we decide to see a movie. We're holdin' hands and everything walkin' to the theater, but stop when we get in line 'cause we're standin' in front of each other. But whatever, I don't make anything of it. But in the movie, she's not touchin' me at all! I put my arm around her, and she doesn't react. But I dunno—is she not feeling me? Or is it just awkward 'cause of those big armrests? So after the movie, I ask if she wants to go to this party with me. She says no and was actin' all weird."

Friend: "Yeah, 'cause of the movie! The fool took her to see *Inception*. Have you seen it? You walk out all tripped out and shit, like what's real, what's fake, what's goin' on? I think she was just bugged out!"

Guy: "Whatever, man, lemme finish. She doesn't wanna go to the party, and I'm crackin' on her a little bit. Not in a mean way, but like, 'Ah, you're lame—come on out with me.' I dunno if she thought it was too forward or I was just tryin' to get on her, or what. So I was like, 'Well at least lemme walk you home.' She lives up this big hill, and we're halfway up when a cab comes. She goes, 'You better take this. There's never any cabs around here.' And I'm thinkin', 'Does she want me to take this cab 'cause she doesn't want me to kiss her when we get to her place?' I dunno what to do, and the cab was there, so I hop in."

"Did you kiss her?"

"Nah, I panicked. Just got in the cab and left. Then this morning I send her a text: 'I had a great time last night it was fun hanging out.' And here's what we've been debating all morning: she wrote back 'I had fun too.' *Smiley face.*"

I was confused for a second. "Wait, what are you debating?"

"The smiley face! What does it mean? She's not the kinda girl who types smiley faces all the time, ya know? I'd say in all our texting she's sent maybe . . . two? Don't you think that's gotta be a sign she likes me? That's flirty, right? You're a girl. What do you think?"

I suddenly felt ridiculous for every time I've asked one of my guy friends for advice "from a guy's perspective." Like they're supposed to have some great insight into a guy they've never met just because they have a penis.

"Man, I have no idea what it means. I'm sorry. I've never thought about it because I guess I don't really use smiley faces."

"Exactly. Neither does she! So it's gotta mean something."

I think you could have asked every person in the park that day what these two guys were talking about, and not one would even come close. All of the ridiculous things that girls spend forever analyzing . . . guys do it too. Grown men, dressed like thugs and drinking 40s, no less, were analyzing every second of a date and spending their afternoon trying to find the deeper meaning in an emoticon.

It's moments like these that gave me faith: the warm, fuzzy feeling that things aren't nearly as bad as we imagine. We're so used to being pitted against men, being told they're the bad guys, and being threatened by ways they might use us, discard us, and leave us in pieces. And then something like this happens, and it's a giant leveler; a gentle reminder that despite all we've been told, it's not us versus them—we're all in this together.

As women we have this idea that guys don't care, or just aren't that emotionally invested in relationships. We think they're these sex-seeking tin men who are destined to never find their hearts. We suspect we can't trust them because their biology has made them remorseless snakes. And we believe this because these are the depictions that are constantly being shoved in our faces.

Some of the most popular shows in America are sitcoms that

feature sex-hungry, emotionally stunted men like *How I Met Your Mother*, *Rules of Engagement*, *Two and a Half Men*, and *Family Guy*. Many commercials for beer, chips, fast food, soda, you name it, are built entirely around the idea that guys are constantly just trying to get some. The 2011 Super Bowl ad for Pepsi Max shows the inner monologue of a couple on a first date, and the guy's thoughts are simply: "I want to sleep with her, I want to sleep with her, I want to sleep with her . . ." Then, there are Tucker Max's best-selling memoirs about all the funny ways he got drunk and screwed over girls, *I Hope They Serve Beer in Hell*, and its sequel, *Assholes Finish First*. And you can't even read the news without hearing about how much men suck. A recent article on CNN.com titled "Men Have Upper Hand in Sexual Economy" was based on the work of Mark Regnerus and Jeremy Uecker, who have decided (ridiculously) that since guys can jerk off to porn, they no longer desire relationships with women.[1]

Our biggest relationship fears, most debasing sexual stereotypes, and worst dating experiences are constantly being reaffirmed as simply "how guys are." Because when you look at the portrayals of men across the media, all signs point to asshole.

But what if the media has it wrong? What if the popular ideas that guys will do anything for sex, don't care about girls as people, and are virtually incapable of emotional intimacy are actually a sales angle more than a reflection of reality? What if, like the useless info-products on the Home Shopping Network, they're selling it because we're buying it? And we're buying it not only because it fits in with the images of men that have surrounded us our entire lives, but because it helps us explain past failed relationships with one soothing generalization: Guys are assholes.

But the thing is: They aren't. It's the truth that social scientists have been screaming now for decades: This image we're shown of "guys" isn't how they really are or how they really think. Men find comfort in relationships,[2] they fall in love faster,[3] and fall out of love harder.[4] They want to get married![5] They won't pursue sex above all else, and there will actually be times they're not in the mood to do it.[6] They may not always show it, but guys have feelings and yearn for emotional connection and companionship.[7]

Holy shit: Guys are people! Despite the headlines in popular magazines that would suggest otherwise, guys are fully functioning human beings who aren't actually all that different from girls.[8]

The trouble is, in order to get an accurate picture of men's feelings, you have to look in psychology textbooks or scholarly journals. Academic publications on gender psychology, intimate relationships, and human sexuality—journals like *Men and Masculinities*, *Psychological Bulletin*, and *Sex Roles*—they're all filled with exhaustive, large-scale studies and meta-analyses showing men have needs that extend much further than their penises. And yet, mainstream media is still obsessed with supporting this single stereotypical (and narrow) image of what "men" are supposedly like because it fits in with our cultural norms and expectations.

But the worst part is, it's not just the media that depend on these misinformed ideas. For the most part, the multi-million-dollar self-help dating industry relies on them just as heavily, and gives relationship advice—to men and women—based on false assumptions about men's psyches. The result is "self help" that is entirely unhelpful, if not completely counterproductive.

When a guy needs help with the ladies, here are his book choices: *The Professional Bachelor's Dating Guide*, *The Game*, *Get Laid Now*, *Player's Handbook*, *The Mystery Method*, and *The Lay Guide*. The titles alone suggest that if he's interested in dating, he has to mask it in the idea he's just looking to get some action. The books them-

selves preach that if he wants to get girls, he should be overly confident and emotionally vacant. *The Mystery Method*, which was
immortalized in Neil Strauss's *The Game* and spun off into the
VH-1 reality series *The Pickup Artist*, goes even further by recom-
mending a guy ignore the girl he's actually interested in. Then,
says Mystery (the pickup artist behind this pearl of wisdom), you
should "neg" her. (For those of you not well versed in pickup culture lingo, a *neg* is a playful insult.) The summary: As a guy, your
interest in women should revolve around getting laid, and if you
want a girl to like you, you have to act emotionless, and pretend
that you don't really like her.

Then, this stellar advice that's given to guys carries over into
books for women that supposedly explain men's "inner thoughts
and feelings." Titles like *He's Just Not That into You* claim if he's not
sleeping with you, he doesn't like you. (Because *all* guys want is
sex, of course.) Steve Harvey's *Act Like a Lady, Think Like a Man*
says you can't ask a guy out or you'll ruin "the chase." (Because guys
always want to be the ones facing rejection . . . since they could
never *actually* be emotionally invested in a woman.) *The Rules*
is an elaborate play-by-play on how to manipulate a guy into pro-
posing. (Since marriage is *never* something a guy would want on
his own.) And *The Manual* even goes so far as to explain "the myth
of the nice guy." (Which wasn't actually a myth until he read some
stupid dating book telling him he has to be a jerk in order for you
to like him.) In our ironically twisted sex, dating, and relationship
culture, we sell books to guys telling them that in order to get girls,
they have to be assholes. And then, we sell books to girls explaining
how to cope with the inevitability of guys' "natural" inclination to
treat girls like shit.

All these books that are supposed to help you decipher guys . . .

just don't. Because they aren't based in the reality of guy experience; they're based in guy myth. And this cultivated distrust of men that we think might be protective actually just gets in our way. Believing guys are jerks makes them more intimidating, obscures our analysis of dating situations, and gives us less power in relationships.

As a relationship expert, cognitively I've long known that guys aren't even a quarter as bad as we give them credit for. I studied human sexuality and intimate relationships in college, and now I write sexual health books and articles, and have made a living traveling around the country speaking on college campuses about sex and relationships. The fact that guys are actual feeling human beings is something I've written and lectured about repeatedly.

The problem was, on a personal level, damn it if all the TV shows, pop psychology, cultural stereotypes, and even a few of my own bad experiences hadn't taken their toll. Even though my brain knew that guys are (for the most part) trustworthy, sensitive beings, somewhere deep inside, my gut didn't. I'd read all the literature, but to really believe it, I knew I'd have to see it for myself.

So to put an end to this distrust—not just for me, but for women everywhere—I set out on a journey around the country to ask more than 1,000 men what they really think about sex, love, and dating.

Knowing I couldn't literally travel *all* around the country, I narrowed my quest to ten major cities: Boston, Seattle, San Francisco, Los Angeles, Chicago, Denver, Atlanta, Houston, New York, and Washington, DC. Ten cities with different vibes, spread out around the country, each of them hubs for young professionals.

I'd fly into a city, rent a car, and ask locals what parts of town I should visit in order to get a broad cross section of guys with different careers, backgrounds, and ethnicities. I'd hit up fast-food joints, office courtyards, parks, coffee shops, bars, and harass guys literally anywhere I could find them. At times I was adopted by strangers and let into office buildings, house parties, fund-raisers, or pub crawls. In Houston I met some guys who snuck me into a Texan's tailgate for the meager price of a case of beer. In Chicago, I scored a ticket to the final day of Lollapalooza—which, in hind-sight, probably wasn't the best place to be asking guys to fill out surveys about their dating lives. But trust me, when I say ALL types of guys were interviewed for this book, I really mean it. So whatever your "type" is, you can rest assured that plenty of them were included.

In each city I had two goals. First: find guys willing to talk with me about love, sex, girls, dating, relationships, and any other juicy tidbits. Second: beg, lie, steal, do whatever it might take to get 150 surveys filled out. The survey I created is 40 questions about hook-ups, dating, and relationships, and it's in the back of this book if you want to take a peek.

To qualify for the survey, a guy couldn't be gay, married, or engaged, because I thought that my data should come from guys you could theoretically start dating. The other requirement was no full-time college students. I wanted to talk to guys once they were in the real world, not the land of "I'll get a keg, throw it in my shit-covered basement, and see what girl falls on my dick." For the most part, the guys who filled out the survey were 21 or older. I didn't set an official age cap, but I didn't speak to men in their 50s and spoke to very few over 40.

Armed (with surveys) and dangerous, I terrorized the country in intense four-day spurts. When I wasn't being escorted out of places (which happened quite often), I was confronting the challenge of getting guys to agree to take the survey. It probably helped that I massaged the truth a bit about the length: "It only takes five minutes" (in reality, it took 10 to 20). But there were a lot of guys who were actually excited about filling it out. A guy in Boston responded eagerly: "Whenever I hear things about men thinking this or doing that, I always feel like, 'How come nobody asks me what I think?' Hell yes, I'll take this survey!"

From excited to confused, I got all sorts of reactions. Some guys were surprised when I'd whip out the clipboard because they thought my preamble was just an intricate pickup line ("oh, you seriously have a survey"). Others were suspicious it was a trap set up by their girlfriends. Many thought it was all an elaborate scheme to find myself a boyfriend. And one guy who had just accepted a job at the FBI thought this might be another test. But the most common response was: What did some guy do to you? They all assumed I had had some terrible experiences with men and was out to prove how much they sucked. Many of them nearly guessed the title too. I heard this a lot: "What are you going to call this book? *Guys Are Assholes*?" They were all shocked when I told them afterward that I actually wanted to prove guys weren't that bad.

But no matter what comments they had about the survey going in, after a few questions, most got really into it. They'd say things like: "Whoa, this is deep, I've never thought about this stuff before . . . It's really made me reevaluate my current situation." Others actually got offended by the questions, complaining: "Why are you automatically assuming I'm going to be a jerk?" Even groups seemingly made up of obnoxious cheese dicks would get quiet as they moved through the questionnaire—like dragons who had been lulled into a sleepy stupor. Of course, some groups (mostly the ones in bars) needed constant babysitting to make sure that they were filling it out by themselves, and that they had the stamina to make it through all three pages.

Sometimes, the people who needed the most babysitting were the girls who were hanging out with the guys taking the survey. In a particularly hostile environment in Wash Park in Denver, I had a girl in one group tell me I was ruining her party, girls in another grabbing the clipboards out of the guys' hands, and then a girl in yet another group get in my face screaming obscenities after discovering her boyfriend was filling out a questionnaire. Hands down, it was the closest I've ever been to getting my ass kicked.

Needless to say, I threw out the crazy girl's boyfriend's questionnaire. I also threw out any others completed by guys whose girlfriends were hovering over their shoulders monitoring the answers, as well as those filled out by guys who clearly didn't take it seriously. Though at the time it wasn't always obvious who was making a joke out of it and who wasn't, the answers usually spoke for themselves. Guys who weren't willing to be honest would write their occupation as "Professional Dick," say their biggest date turnoff was "farts," or say they treat a girl differently if they want a relationship with her by "not cumming on her face." Other than those very few, I really do think the guys who took the time to fill out the survey answered honestly . . . or at least as honestly as they answer to themselves.

And so that, in a nutshell, was my 10-city man-trek. By the end of it, I had lost my wallet, my keys, my boyfriend of two years, and a box of 450 surveys I collected in Boston, Seattle, and San Francisco. (The stats in this book are based on 750 surveys from New York, LA, Denver, Chicago, and Atlanta. After losing the surveys from three cities, I decided to use the data from the five geographically diverse cities I had already visited, and just focus on verbal interviews during my two remaining trips—to Houston and DC. I also created a follow-up survey that 200 guys filled out online. So, overall, I actually spoke with well over 1,000 guys.) I'm exhausted. Between the guys I've met around the country and the ones whose dating lives I've been following via monthly phone calls, I feel like I've been involved in the relationships of hundreds of men.

The strangest part of this experience, though, has been the blurring between my work and my personal life. Like a mad scientist, at times I got too close to the project, and if this were a sci-fi movie I basically injected my arm with the experimental serum and turned myself into a werewolf. While studying men, my opinions from my research and my perception of my own relationships were at times inseparable. And now that I'm single and starting to date again, my analysis of situations is both personal and professional . . . which is just sort of sick.

So after all this, what have I discovered? That pretty much everything you've been told about men your entire life is a lie. If dating were a test, you'd be walking into it unprepared because you've been studying the wrong book. You make decisions about sex and relationships completely blind because you've never been told what guys are REALLY thinking. When you actually ask guys themselves—not entertainment executives, middle-aged men and women who write obnoxious self-help books, or so-called dating coaches—some of their seemingly asshole actions make more sense, and dating is a lot more straightforward.

This book will help you understand guys' side of the story, which, I can tell you, looks a lot better than you'd think judging simply by the cover. Consider the rest of this book proof that—for the most part—guys are thinking, feeling beings who want to be in relationships.

Boston: "I'm Not Most Guys"

Fresh on my man-stalking mission, I went to Boston Commons to hit up businessmen having lunch in the park. Not only did I find survey takers, I also ran into Daniel, a guy friend I've known since middle school, dressed up in a colonial outfit giving a guided tour. We decided to meet for a late lunch.

Daniel is a tall good-looking guy with the most pronounced duck walk you've ever seen. He waddled in, still dressed to the nines in his white ruffled shirt, long brown tuxedo jacket, bloomers, and knee socks, and caught me up on the last few years. He told me about the girlfriend he's living with who has a six-year-old son. He loves his girlfriend and, by extension, her kid. He has been playing the role of the father figure, and recounted an elaborate story about disciplining the boy by threatening to leave his popsicles out in the blazing heat and taking away his video games. When I told him more about my book, he launched into his theories about relationships, ending with: "It's just not in guys' nature to be monogamous."

Not in their nature to be monogamous? This from a 26-year-old guy who's living with his girlfriend and acting like a father to her son? Prior to that, he was with the same girl for eight years, since junior year of high school. During the year or so in between he was a shit show, and clearly couldn't function without a girl in his life. So this was really an interesting theory to be coming from him: the poster child for long-term monogamous relationships.

Trying to understand his point better, I had to ask: "But

you've been nothing but monogamous! I mean, have you ever even cheated?"

He thought about it for a second. "Well, yeah. In ninth grade . . . when I was dating you. I made out with this girl on the beach and then came home and broke up with you."

Daniel and I dated for three months when we were both 14. "That's right! I forgot you cheated on me! And dumped me on Christmas Eve or something too, jerk off!"

We had joked about this incident in the past, but I had forgotten. Though I'm sure I would have been horrified at the time, our "relationship" was one of those early high school ones that seem to occur in a different lifetime. I couldn't care less that he cheated on me, but on the other hand, not exactly a high note to be starting my research on—a reminder that my first boyfriend made out with some girl and then dumped me on Christmas Eve.

But all 14-year-old drama aside, why would a guy who's never pursued anything other than a long-term relationship—and whose sketchiest boyfriend move was kissing another girl on the beach when he was 14—believe that men are not made for monogamy?

Situations like this one came up again and again. Guys have countless theories about how "guys" act and feel. But if asked, "Is that how *you* feel?" or "Is that *your* experience?" they often reply, "No . . . but I'm not most guys."

It's strange, because typically, we work the other way around. Your theories on life, right or wrong, are gross generalizations based on your own feelings and experiences. Why is it that this particular topic would buck the trend? Why are guys so completely convinced other guys feel things that they themselves do not? In fact, they'll even claim other guys feel things that are the total *opposite* of what they do. It just doesn't add up. But what it implies is that guys are completely clueless about other guys. And often, when they speak on behalf of "guys" as a group, they come up with answers that are entirely off base.

"A Fake Reputation Is All a Man Has"

UNLEARNING "GUYS"

We hold these truths to be self-evident, that all men are created equal, that they are born void of all emotional needs, that they want sex more than anything else in the world, and that they desire to stay as uncommitted as possible.

All guys are assholes. It's a belief we hold near and dear to our hearts. It's why they just want sex, why they don't want to be your boyfriend, and why they're destined to cheat with the nanny. We think we know these things about men as well as we know the facts of history or anything else—hell, as far as we're concerned, guys' jerkishness might as well be written into the Declaration of Independence. But what if . . . we don't actually know men at all?

Chris Owens teaches a human sexuality class at a community college outside of Portland. He's taught this class on and off since the '70s and starts each semester by separating the students into a male group and a female group and asking them what the other gender wants sexually. "It used to be that guys didn't have a clue," he told me. "Now, it's the girls who are more out of touch with male desires. They say guys want oral sex, and guys want sexual variety. And the guys in the class see the girls' list and say, 'We want relationships.' And that's something the female group either neglects to think of or state when reporting their assessment of male desires."

What I'm about to reveal to you about men probably runs completely counter to everything you *think* you know about them. It's probably the biggest cover-up in United States history, and I may be assassinated for divulging the truth: Guys aren't assholes; they're giant pussies.

And I mean that in the best possible way.

Nearly every psychologist will agree with the earth-shattering idea that the majority of men want an emotional connection with women.[1] Men—get this—enjoy relationships. When they're in them, they're more fulfilled, they're physically[2] and mentally healthier,[3] they live longer,[4] and they're more content with their lives.[5] In my own research, I found that the overwhelming majority of guys are looking for a girlfriend rather than simply a girl to sleep with. I found that guys worry about impressing girls, being vulnerable, and falling in love first. They analyze how we act and what we say, and get hurt when we do something insensitive. And they care about more than just sex—even if that's not always how they behave.

You read it here first, ladies: You will not inevitably get screwed over by a guy. You do not have to act uninterested in a relationship and only pursue sex in order to "not scare him off." You are not destined to need him more than he needs you.

Guys aren't jerks. And once you learn what they're really thinking, you'll have more confidence when meeting them, you'll be better equipped to understand their actions, and you'll know how to proceed in all dating/relationship/hookup scenarios. But before we go into specifics, I want to clear up a few general misconceptions.

Are Guys Assholes Because They're from Mars?

Are men and women different? Of course. I could have told you that by pulling down my pants. Are we so different that we should be talked about like we're from two different planets? Probably not. These are some of the things we know about the differences between men and women: Men have penises; women have vaginas. Men are generally taller and have greater muscle mass. Men and women have different levels of certain hormones. But psychologically speaking, when looking at the bulk of the data, for the most part, men and women are pretty similar.[6] Not only that, but the differences *within* each sex are much greater than the differences *between* the sexes.[7]

That's right, guys' and girls' minds are pretty much the same. Which is sort of a tough pill to swallow—especially given all of the biological differences we always seem to be hearing about. You wouldn't be in the minority if you've been led to believe that guys' and girls' brains are simply hardwired to have different drives. That it's just how we're programmed: You know, I'm a Mac; he's a PC.

But, in fact, not only are guys' and girls' minds pretty similar psychologically, they're pretty similar biologically as well. In her book *Pink Brain, Blue Brain,* neuroscientist Lise Eliot, Ph.D., looked at the brains of little boys and little girls. And after an exhaustive search of available literature, she found "surprisingly little evidence of sex differences in children's brains." She didn't find any real differences (and the ones that surfaced were mostly small) until she looked at the brains of adults. This is significant, she explains, because of a phenomenon called plasticity. Plasticity is the fact that brains change based on your experiences. So grown men's brains may look a little different from ours, but that's at least in part because of what they've learned in 20-some years of growing up as guys.[8]

Most important, though, hardwired or not, there's no proof that these small brain differences would cause men to think, feel, and act in ways that we do not. "The truth is," says Cynthia Kuhn, Ph.D., a neurobiologist who studies sex differences in the brain, "there are many differences between male and female brains, especially regarding reproductive functions, but it's impossible to prove how these structural differences would account for different feelings, attitudes, or behaviors—there are many other factors at play, including family and the larger social environment. Brains are complex—you can't single out one little difference and say it's the reason a guy might act a certain way. Although modern imaging shows the activity of brains, this activity can reflect both underlying neural structure and changes caused by learning."[9]

Differences in men and women's brains cannot be conclusively linked to differences in men and women's desires or behaviors. And yet, that won't stop books and articles from claiming that they can. Why? Because it makes a good story. It seemingly explains catcalls from construction workers, why you fought with your ex, and why that dickhead didn't call you back after you slept with him.

But though these ideas about the underlying biological causes of men's behaviors are often presented as facts, they're actually just unproven hypotheses. "Some are plucked out of thin air because they sound about right," says Eliot. "Others are cherry-picked from single studies or extrapolated from rodent research without any effort to critically evaluate all the data, account for conflicting studies, or even state that the results have never been confirmed in humans."[10] Basically, you may open the newspaper to a story about men acting or feeling one way or another based on a study of male rats, an interesting and yet irrelevant scientific factoid, or the freak result of research that actually stands in stark contrast with the majority of the data on that same topic.

I know, I'm sorry. The belief that our relationship troubles can be traced back to men's subpar biology is one that's hard to give up. "Your boyfriend is insensitive because a chunk of his brain is missing"—that just sounds good, doesn't it? It sounds a hell of a lot better than this: Relationships are tough. It's hard enough to live in a way that you don't let yourself down, not to mention another person. People have the ability to be incredibly selfish, take others for granted, and act irresponsibly with another's emotions. Santa Claus doesn't exist, soft pretzels have almost 800 calories, and romantic relationships are tough because they are—not because men and women are so fundamentally incompatible.

Are Guys Assholes Because They Have to Spread Their Seed?

A guy's got to spread his seed. How often have you heard that one? The theory goes something like this: As David M. Buss explains in *The Handbook of Evolutionary Psychology*, guys are inclined to sleep around because "a man can produce as many as 100 offspring by mating with 100 women over the course of a year, whereas a man who is monogamous tends to have only one child with his partner during that time." For that reason, men have a natural "desire for sexual variety" and "short-term partners." And there you have it. The gold card for a guy who wants to sleep around: "But, babe, I can't help evolution."

Nice try. But this idea is suspect for many reasons. For one, it doesn't explain the fact that humans have sex at times when pregnancy isn't possible. Or that even historically, we have gone to lengths to actually prevent it (ancient cave paintings that date back to AD 100 show evidence of condom use).[11] So at least for the last 1,900 years, sex has been about more than just reproduction.

More practically, however (as just discussed), the brain adapts based on its surroundings. So in this day and age, with child support and what not, what guy actually wants to father hundreds of babies? I mean, wouldn't that be a giant pain in his ass? And if this is really what guys wanted, wouldn't they be alternating trips to the club with trips to the sperm bank? You know, hedge their bets?

Alas, the proof is in the pudding—what do guys say they want? Do most actually want their romantic lives to consist of a flurry of one-night stands? To test this question, David Buss (the guy behind the "spread the seed" theories) and his colleague David Schmit asked 150 undergraduates how many sexual partners they desired in the next 30 years. They found that, on average, guys wanted 16, while girls wanted four, a stat that would support their hypothesis.

But here's the problem. When analyzing students' responses Buss and Schmit took the average (the mean) instead of looking at the median (the number in the middle if you line up all the answers highest to lowest). Looking at the average is problematic when you have a few dudes who walked into the study (possibly still drunk from the night before) and wrote that they want to be with 100 women. When this study was repeated by other researchers, and they instead looked at the medians (because, as predicted, there were more "100 plus" outlier answers given by guys), there was no significant difference between the number of people men and women wanted to have sex with.

This is yet another example of why it's important to know that the results of one study are not by any means the full story. When the media uses a single study to make lofty assumptions, be skeptical. Ask, how many people were involved? How were the results measured? And even, what *kind* of people were involved? A good majority of psychological research is based on undergraduate college students. And I think most guys (and girls!) would tell you their attitudes and life goals may have matured a bit since their "drink over the sink till you puke" undergraduate days.

So if most guys don't actually just want to spread their seed, what do they want? According to one study, 98.9% of them want to settle down with one exclusive partner in their lifetime, preferably within the next five years.[12] The research I did backed this up too. Of the guys I surveyed, 95% said that they want to get married some day. And 99% of them said that if the right girl came around, they would want to be in a relationship with her. Despite the attention that the "seed spreading" theories have gotten, it seems that another evolutionary story is more correct: that men are driven to pair bond, just like women.[13]

If Biology and Evolution Aren't Making Guys Assholes, What Is?

Let's take a second to look at the big picture of what it's like to grow up as a dude. Guys (like girls) begin receiving messages about how they should behave from the second they come out of the womb and get dressed in blue. And these messages are everywhere: from parents telling their sons not to cry[14] to grade school text-books that overwhelmingly show boys as aggressive, argumenta-tive, and competitive,[15] to male role models on TV who skateboard recklessly or launch themselves hundreds of feet into the air in shopping carts. It's clear: Being a boy means you're not supposed to show weakness, fear, or any type of vulnerability.

As far as romantic expectations go, guys are told that being a man means having sex, not relationships. Ronald Levant, Ed.D., who has been studying masculinity since the late '80s, says, "Sadly there hasn't been much of a shift in social norms since then. First of all, we believe that men should always want sex, and never turn it down. Over 100 studies in the past 20 years continue to show this as well as the fact that our cultural expectation is for men to take a non-relational approach to sexuality—basically, have sex void of any emotion." But this is not what guys actually want, or how they actually feel. Niobe Way, Ph.D., who also studies masculin-ity, wrote *Deep Secrets* based on her interviews with 600 guys. She

concludes that as boys become men, they feel pressured to aban-
don the emotional connections they yearn for because our society
sees feelings and emotions as things that are "gay" or "feminine."
The cultural message sent loud and clear is this: Real men don't have
emotional needs and shouldn't pursue relationships, because that's
"gay." What "real men" should do is get laid all the time.

The sad truth is, even though we don't want guys to be these
sex-seeking apes, as women, we're guilty of perpetuating these expectations. How often have you heard a girl say, "I'm sort of the
guy in the relationship because I'm not that emotionally invested"?
Or have you ever been in a situation where you wanted to have
sex and a guy didn't? Then it's, "I wonder what's wrong with him?
Maybe his dick is really small? Or he has trouble getting it up? Or
maybe he's gay?"

And of course, men are also guilty for using these standards to
judge each other. 50 Cent—the rapper responsible for the literary
gold "You don't have to take your panties off, just move 'em to the
side"—is someone most guys probably consider to be a badass.
John Mayer, on the other hand, the singer/songwriter behind "Your
body is a wonderland," he's a pussy. Well, he was, until he gave
sexually explicit interviews about doing Jessica Simpson. Now, after
acting sexually irresponsible, I bet many guys would bump him up
to badass status (or at least bump him out of the "pussy" caste).

When guys don't conform to the stereotypical male image, they
don't just judge each other, they judge themselves. The Pepsi Max
advertisement mentioned earlier in the book is posted on a website
over it's explanation: "As with every first date, this guy has only
one thing on his mind." The first comment on the page is from a
guy who wrote, "Am I effeminate for not being like that?" And I
wonder, is the fact that this guy wasn't sex-obsessed something that

he'd be willing to admit in front of his guy friends? Or only anonymously on a website?

Even if it's not true, many guys will act like they just want sex and are uninterested in relationships. They have to. Because when they don't conform to our cultural norms, they're made to feel ashamed.[16]

If Guys Aren't Assholes, Why Do They Think They Are?

When I was working on this book, I went home for a bit and ran into my dad's friend Jerry early one morning at Whole Foods. He was with his "breakfast club," a group of guys who meet literally *every* morning for breakfast. The club has strict rules. From 7 o'clock to 8 o'clock, no talking; they sit at different tables, drink their coffee, and read the paper. Then at 8 o'clock they gather at one table and start yapping. Apparently, the rules are no joke—guys have actually gotten "kicked out" for violating them and talking too soon.

I told Jerry I was working on a book about guys, and that a basic premise was the idea that men and women have similar relationship needs. He was quick to disagree with me, saying that men—even older men—are "constantly horny." (I can't begin to tell you how disturbing it is to be in a conversation with one of your parents' friends that involves the word *horny*.) His proof for this assertion was that every morning he and the rest of the breakfast club ogle the cashiers who come in wearing "painted-on jeans."

"But really, Amber, can you see a bunch of women doing that? Ogling the cashiers every day?"

"I don't know, Jerry." I panicked. My mom had gotten involved in the conversation too, was also dropping the h-word, and I had to get out as quickly as possible. But over the next few days, I thought about what he said. Would a bunch of older ladies sit around ogling young men? Maybe not. But because they aren't horny, or because . . . because they don't have to!

"Dad!" I ran out of my room screaming. "I figured it out!"

"What mutual fund to invest your Roth IRA in?"

"No, why Jerry and his friends ogle at the cashiers! It's because they're afraid it looks gay. The breakfast club . . . it's a bunch of guys who meet up every morning because they need the companionship. There's no sports, no drinking, just men meeting up, reading the paper, sipping their coffee, like some married couple or . . . freaky . . . group . . . thing? Or something. But the point is, stereotypically speaking, this isn't a very 'manly' thing to do. So to make each other feel more comfortable, they have to show how straight they are by talking about 'painted-on jeans.' Otherwise, the other little boys on the playground might run around saying, 'You meet a group of guys every morning to drink fair-trade coffee, eat organic eggs, and just chat? That's so gay.'"

As Dr. Michael Kimmel concludes in his book *Guyland:* "Masculinity is a homosocial experience, performed for, and judged by, other men." And this is where it all comes full circle. You have a bunch of guys running around feeling like they're *supposed* to act like indiscriminate horndogs. They put up this front because if they don't, they're afraid they'll be ridiculed. And the outcome then is that guys *actually* believe this is how men truly are, because it's how they've seen their peers act their entire lives. Many become convinced that other guys are acting out their authentic feelings when they act like freewheeling sex fiends. So even if a guy knows that he himself does not represent the stereotypical image of a "guy," he remains thoroughly convinced that the other guys around him do.

This misunderstanding many men have about themselves is one of the most confusing parts of the idea that guys aren't assholes—the fact that so many of them will say "guys" (as a group) are. Thirty-five percent of guys who filled out my survey said they'd lie in order to sleep with a girl. But a full 87% believed "most guys" would. Only 15% of guys said, romantically speaking, they were jerks to girls. But 54% of them thought guys in general were. How do men's thoughts about themselves as a group affect you? Like this: Have you ever gotten advice about a guy from one of your male friends? "Oh he's probably cheating on you. Or he's just trying to get laid. Or he's bound to screw you over in some other way because he's a dirtbag. Trust me on this one, I'm a dude, I know." But ironically, they don't.

If It's All a Show, Why Do Guys Keep Up the Asshole Act?

You would think that if guys aren't actually as bad as they're made out to be, they'd rise up and revolt. Like feminism, but masculin-ism. Why aren't guys taking to the airwaves explaining, "Hey, we're not the scum everybody thinks we are?"

Consider this: Masculinity as it's currently constructed (strong, emotionless, and fearless) is a role that comes with a lot of power and privilege[17] (the presidency, heading up large companies, and a general air of capability). And in intimate relationships, this asshole stereotype gives men a huge amount of control.

If you don't give a shit, you aren't vulnerable. If you aren't vulnerable, you have the upper hand. A male acquaintance said to me in college: "Why would a guy admit he likes a girl, ask her out on a date, and risk rejection? When instead, he could just try to hook up with her, and if she rejects him, then he's not as exposed?" If guys were more up-front about the fact that they want more than just sex, it would give us power by exposing their emotional vulnerability, and the reality that we're in the position to hurt them. But having us think guys don't have feelings gives the illusion they control relationships, because we want them and they don't. It's like the Wizard of Oz. Hiding behind this scary asshole image, men seem so intimidating. If they were to pull back the curtain, we'd see they're not these mighty assholes; they're just vulnerable guys clutching their joysticks.

So instead of trying to fight their sleazy reputation, many guys embrace it. And worst of all, some think it's the only way that we'll like them. Yes, many guys believe that girls love assholes. As one guy put it: "I don't always act like a jerk to girls. But I do notice that some girls like jerks. So if I catch that vibe, I can alter to more jerky." Another one said: "I've been nice and it's been a mistake. Jerkiness works." And yet another admitted: "I hate the games we all play, but I play them anyways. I hate that the asshole gets the girl and the nice guy gets screwed." We can blame pickup methods, girls who like bad boys, or our society's screwed-up ideas about what it means to be a man. But whatever the cause, many guys think that if they don't act like jerks, they're at a serious dating disadvantage.

This is where the idea that guys *aren't* assholes gets a bit tricky. What I mean is, guys aren't biologically programmed to be any worse (romantically speaking) than girls are. And honestly, even if they were, biology is never the full story, as humans have adapted to be able to control their unsavory impulses. If a guy can resist the urge to club his boss over the head in hopes of taking over his position, he can resist the urge to sleep with every woman he sees (if that urge even exists in the first place).

The tricky part is, guys have grown up in a culture that tells them they're assholes. They've grown up with researchers who have given them scientific justification for why they are. Their male role models in the media are for the most part sex hungry, commitment avoiding, and emotionally vacant. Many have friends who reflect that idea of manhood on the outside, even if it's not what they're feeling on the inside. And the pressure that guys feel to live up to their asshole persona can be great. All of these things, understandably, have confused guys and left some acting like assholes because they haven't quite figured out they don't have to be.

Doing research for this book, I read *The Game*, a guide for men pickup artists and (supposedly) how to get laid. It was riveting, and if you haven't read it, you need to. It's about all these guys who spend tons of money and hours of training learning how to get girls to have casual sex with them. Then, the relationships these guys develop with each other become just as tumultuous and complex as romantic ones. So even though they may have been avoiding relationships with women, they ended up having sex with women, and then emotional relationships with one another. And by the end, they all pretty much realized they wanted girlfriends. So this book, with its faux-leather cover, gold-leaf pages, and Hugh Hefner–wannabe description, ultimately boiled down to being about how men need emotional connection.

This is such a metaphor for the male dating experience in general. On the inside it's confused, vulnerable, and emotionally needy. But on the outside it looks intimidating, flashy, and like it's all about sex.

We know what guys look like on the outside. This book is going to get you on the inside. It's going to expose guys' true feelings about dating, sex, and relationships and uncover the thoughts that sometimes even guys themselves were surprised they had. Along the way, you'll find out why they don't call, the signs they like you, the signs they don't, the right time to have sex, what causes problems in relationships, and more. In a larger sense, you'll learn how to decipher dating situations. And by the end, I can promise, you'll never look at guys the same way again.

STOP!

No really, **STOP!**

    Before you read any further, there are some things you have to know about guys. After all of my research, there are three overarching lessons I've learned. And in order for you to make best usage out of the rest of this book, you have to know them too.

LESSON #1: MANY GUYS REGURGITATE SHIT WHEN IT COMES TO TALKING ABOUT GIRLS. AND WHEN YOU REGURGITATE SHIT, YOU SOUND LIKE AN ASSHOLE.

The biggest problem with asking guys to talk about their feelings on sex, love, and dating is that often they're not really sure how they feel. For many, their first instinct is to revert to canned answers and meaningless phrases about how guys are supposed to think. Take, for example, "the chase."

    At a deli in San Francisco I met a man who wasn't in the mood to take the survey, but said he'd answer one question. I went with: "If you sleep with a girl right away, does it mess up the chances of a relationship? And if so, why?"

    "Well that's an easy one," he chuckled. "Yes. Because it ruins the chase."

    I got annoyed: "Can you *please* tell me what that even means?" As many guys had dropped the "chase" card, no one had actually bothered to explain it.

    "I don't know. I guess it's like . . . you don't even know this girl and she's willing to sleep with you. If you don't know her at all, then you just aren't ready for that level of physical intimacy."

"Wait a minute. You're saying 'the chase' ultimately boils down to wanting to get to know a girl emotionally before getting to know her physically?"

"Yeah, you could say that."

I was shocked. The phrase "the chase" always sounded so intimidating. Like as a girl you don't really matter, to guys you're just some elaborate fleshy game. Guys want to catch you only to prove they can, but aren't serious about wanting to keep you. But even though that's what it sounds like, "the chase" is really about something much more vulnerable. In a sexual framework, it stems from the desire to actually get to know a girl before sleeping with her. To earn physical intimacy at a parallel rate to emotional intimacy . . . and that's actually kinda sweet.

Another phrase that came up a lot was "the hunt": the act of going out to meet girls. Leave it to iPhone-toting, Xbox-playing, plasma-TV-watching dudes to all of a sudden think they're cavemen once women get involved. As if the bar scene is actually them running around in loincloths holding spears over their heads.

"Can you talk to me about 'the hunt'?" I asked a financial analyst in DC over his lunch break.

He gawked. "What? Are you a psychologist or something?" What I assumed was an innocent enough question seemed to alarm him. "Okay . . . maybe I'm uncomfortable with myself and I need approval from these women. I need to know they like me, and that they're attracted to me . . . I guess it's a sense of security."

Other guys echoed similar sentiments, though they were a little calmer about it: "You need to know that people want you—it's human nature. The hunt is about wanting to feel wanted."

Wanting to feel wanted, needing validation, sentiments that are completely vulnerable. . . . Refer to it as "the hunt" and suddenly guys can feel like those emotions are powerful instead of insecure. Although the phrase "the hunt" sounds like guys are trying to mount our heads on their walls, in reality, it's their own validation they're after.

Not only will guys instinctively revert to expressions like "the hunt" or "the chase," they'll also mindlessly regurgitate the romantic priorities they're "supposed to have," as opposed to the ones they actually do. A guy I met in Houston told me "guys are done with girls after they sleep with them because sex equals mission accomplished." But when I asked what was more important to him, sex or having a relationship, he immediately answered "a relationship."

"So then mission not accomplished?" I challenged.

"Huh . . . good point." He conceded with the same startled look I saw repeatedly when I pressed closed-off guys to examine their feelings: part confusion, part denial, and part vulnerability. "You mean I'm not a total douche? Say it ain't so."

Male dating lingo is all about taking vulnerable emotions and sensitive priorities and making them seem cold and aggressive. Many guys are quick to talk about "hunting" and "chasing," often without even realizing what it is they're ultimately hunting and chasing after. They may immediately assume everything is about sex, when in reality it's usually more about relationships (be it the one they have with themselves, their friends, or a girl herself).

When you ask guys to talk about sex and dating, you may initially hear things that sound pretty bad. But more often than not, those guys are just repeating the crap they've picked up along the way about men's sexuality. And unsurprisingly, when regurgitating crap, a guy bears a close resemblance to an asshole. But when you press guys, even a little bit, most realize that what's spewing out of their mouths either isn't entirely accurate or, if it is, it isn't actually as bad as it sounds.

LESSON #2: GUYS ARE SCREWED UP WHEN IT COMES TO SEX.

While studying men, my relationship with them (as a gender) has gone through some pretty severe ups and downs. I can definitively say it was when listening to what some thought about sex that I felt the most inclined to spend the rest of my life alone with a collection of cats.

When it comes to sex, many guys just seem confused. Of those I surveyed, 73% said their primary interest in women is someone to have a relationship with. Another 18% said their primary interest in women is companionship or short-term dating (their other choices were "someone to have sex with" and "someone to impress their friends"). So a full 91% of guys are primarily interested in women because they want some sort of personal connection.

And yet, 44% of those same guys said they'd take a girl on a few dates, text her frequently, and fake an interest in her or her life just to have sex with her. And 35% of guys said they'd lie about their relationship intentions in order to sleep with a girl. It just doesn't add up. If most guys admit they're ultimately after relationships (either short- or long-term), why don't they understand that spending their time and energy lying to get girls in bed isn't the most productive way to achieve that? And all end goals aside, why do so many guys think that lying for the purposes of getting laid is okay?

The general sense I got from a good number of these guys was a feeling of entitlement when it comes to sex. If they want something sexual, they should be able to have it, plain and simple. Guys' sketchy sexual behavior is not so much about their inability to control their penises (as it's often painted), as much as their unwillingness to do so. Many thought that deceiving girls in order to sleep with them was just part of "being a guy." A full 87% of those I surveyed said "*most* guys would lie about their relationship intentions in order to sleep with a girl." And this is a sentiment that has been documented repeatedly in other research. According to Ronald Levant's Male Role Norms Inventory, an idea that both men and women commonly subscribe to (and have for years) is that being a "man" means "using any and all means to 'convince' a woman to have sex."[18] If these rock-bottom sexual standards are just considered to be the "male norm," is it any mystery that so many guys don't surpass them? And when they do, do they get rewarded for being "great guys," or does their manhood, and sex drive (and maybe even sexual orientation) get called into question?

Another likely result of our cultural notions of what it means to be a man is that many guys seem literally unaware that sex is something *they* could actually turn down. This is yet another way guys are screwed up in the sex department. Many I spoke with expressed some level of dissatisfaction or disgust with one-night stands or girls who would sleep with them right away. But not *one* guy (whom I talked to, anyway) acknowledged the active role they play in the process. It was like it had never occurred to them they could (or should) take responsibility for themselves and say no to sex even if a girl says yes. So instead, many guys had sex in situations they weren't totally comfortable with, and then the next day blamed the girl instead of thinking: I played a part in letting that happen too.

Guys aren't assholes; they're truly not. On the whole, they're not untrustworthy, emotionally stunted, or callous. And yet, a significant number of guys will be sexually irresponsible. Guys who in another situation might be great boyfriends and husbands, and who are on the whole good people, often seem to have a block when it comes to sex. If there is one time to be suspicious of a guy's motives, it's when you're engaging with him in a purely sexual context (that is, you're hooking up with a guy you don't know that well).

LESSON #3: GUYS ARE ALL DIFFERENT . . . AND THEY ARE VERY DIFFERENT.

Anyone who tries to tell you what "all guys" think or do is completely full of it and has never spent any time actually talking to a variety of guys about their feelings. The seemingly obvious thing we tend to forget is that guys are all different. Really different. Among scientists who study gender, it's widely accepted that the differences among members of each sex are much greater than the differences between the sexes. So much so, in fact, that the latest edition of the textbook *Intimate Relationships* refuses to refer to men and women as the "opposite sex" and instead references them as the "other sex."

If you randomly selected two guys and one girl, it's very possible that one of the guys and the girl would have more similar attitudes than the two guys. This may initially seem hard to believe. That's because all guys are brought up with the same expectations about what it means to be a man, how men should act, and how men should think. So on the surface many guys come across as the same, but underneath they may actually be pretty different.

At a coffee shop in Denver, I had the pleasure of meeting a guy named Daniel Cook. After he finished taking his survey, we talked for nearly an hour about men and masculinity. He's in his late 20s and runs a men's group that gets together for regular meetings to talk about what it means to be a man. They discuss things like the male role models they had growing up, what type of men they aspire to be, how they can use their masculine qualities to improve the world, live with integrity, and have better relationships with the women they date, their friends, and their family. (I asked, and no, it's not all artsy types.) The group is made up of a variety of different men, who all joined for various reasons and are daring to cultivate their nurturing side and be in touch with their feelings. Their common goal: to figure out how to embody masculinity in the most fulfilling and positive way.

I left our conversation elated. Guys are great. Martin Luther King Jr., Mahatma Gandhi, Nelson Mandela, all these Nobel Prize winners, poets, philanthropists . . . And then, not five minutes later . . .

"I'm curious to talk with you about some of these things." An average-looking guy stopped me as I picked up his completed survey.

"Sure." I sat down across the table still starry-eyed—an innocent lamb going in for slaughter.

"First of all, men aren't made for monogamy like women are. We have to spread our seed. It's our biological urge, to have as many children as possible to ensure the survival of our genes."

At first, I gave him the benefit of the doubt: Maybe he just hadn't really thought it through? "Oh, come on, don't you think that we've evolved a bit? And no guy *actually* wants to impregnate tons of different women."

"No. I think deep down guys have sex wanting to get the girl pregnant. Then they want to move on to another girl and score with as many as possible while remaining completely uncommitted."

No. Nooooo!!!! My newfound love and trust in all things male was slipping through my fingers like sand . . . and he kept going: "Girls like overly cocky guys. Like really jerky, narcissistic guys. When I think of the friends of mine who get the most ass, it's the ones who are the most obnoxious. This one friend of mine is just totally arrogant. But I went to Vegas with him and he slept with four girls in 24 hours. Four girls! That's skill."

Now I was just pissed. "Well, do the cocky friends of yours who get so much ass also happen to be the most good-looking?"

"Maybe. But girls don't think like that. They aren't that shallow. They wouldn't talk to a guy because of his looks. Looks just don't matter that much to them. They want power."

And, faith demolished. How was it that 10 minutes earlier, in the same city, same area of town, even the same coffee shop, I could be talking to another guy of similar age and education (who was even dressed the same way), and their thoughts could be so vastly different?

Even the way guys reacted after taking the survey was completely varied. Some said it was the most reflective thing that they had ever done: "That was tough. It made me really think about my actions." Others thought it was completely juvenile: "What are you, in fifth grade? These were the most irrelevant and immature questions."

At a bar in Venice Beach, I actually got yelled at by a man in his late 30s: "What is this crap?" He waved the survey violently around in the air. "How do you ever expect to understand something as complex as relationships through a written survey? You're going about this all wrong. It's not men are this, women are that; that's why relationships are so hard in the first place. We go into them with preconceived notions that someone must be one way because he's a man, or another way because she's a woman. We need to talk to each other as people, two people, not 'you man' and 'me woman.'"

And the guy was right. After all of my research, there is only one thread I can definitively say ties all men together—and it's probably not what you think. It's not that all guys watch porn (77%), or that their primary interest in women is someone to have sex with (8%). All my blood, sweat, and tears and the only statement I can definitively make about ALL men is that they would want to be in a relationship if the right girl came along (or 99.2% of them, anyway).

Guys aren't all the same. Which is unfortunately problematic given the fact this is a book about how they think, act, and feel. But while it's impossible to say all men think one way or another, if we look at specific situations, there are likely a small handful of reasons a guy may be acting a certain way. And even though all guys are different, very few resemble the stereotypical image we have of "a guy." The first step to correctly assessing your guy situations is double-checking yourself when you're jumping to a conclusion based on your preconceived notions of "men." So here's to unlearning, and seeing situations the way guys *actually* do. Which, in fact, isn't often that different from how we see them ourselves.

Seattle: No Douchey Part of Town

Seattle was the second city I visited, and—since I used to live in Boston—the first one I was unfamiliar with. I relied heavily on friends (and then strangers) to tell me which areas of town, parks, coffee shops, bars, etc., would give me a diverse sampling of Seattle men.

Wherever I was, I learned that there were always more guys "somewhere else." After surveying a handful of guys, I'd ask one if he had a good recommendation for where I might find some more. And no matter where I was, I'd hear: "Yeah, this isn't the best place to be. I'd maybe try [some area of town at least a mile and a half away]." More often than not, it would be an area I just came from. I fell for this at first, and spent hours zigzagging across town, which made for some long and exhausting days. Finally, I learned to just stay put. No guys think the places they hang out have guys in them. Maybe it's because they don't notice them? Or because they don't want to think they hang out in giant sausage fests? Who knows?

My third day, I realized that I was missing a major demographic. Even though I had been all over town, I had somehow missed the douchey crowd—the popped collar, my-daddy-owns-a-yacht, "I don't treat girls like people" types. This started a two-day epic search for the D-bag guys of Seattle.

I started asking strangers, "Can you point me in the direction of a happy hour bar where I might be able to find some real douchebags?" They must have thought I was feeling incredibly self-destructive. Or maybe that I was a suicide bomber. Whatever they thought, though, most would give me a list of four or five bars. I'd go to the bars, talk to some guys, but even when they initially looked like they might fit the bill, they'd end up redeeming themselves.

It would start out so promising too. They'd make some dumb sex joke, or say something macho and annoying, but then when they started really talking, it would turn out they were pretty decent men. As soon as they made this turn, they would see the disappointment creep onto my face.

"What's wrong? I thought you wanted to talk about relationships and stuff?"

"Yeah, no. It's fine." I'd tuck my pen and journal back into my bag. "I just . . . I was kinda looking to talk to a douchebag, that's all. I'm sorry. I gotta go." And with that "It's not you, it's me" breakup, I'd venture to yet another bar, only to have a similar disappointment.

The morning I left Seattle, I left a note and a stack of 20 surveys on the kitchen counter of the friend I had been staying with:

"I had a lot of trouble finding douchey guys. I tried Belltown, bars on Pike, outside the Mariners stadium, and all your other usual suspects. Someone told me Kirkland might be promising? If you have any time in the coming months would you mind taking these surveys to the douchiest bar you can think of? Thanks so much for letting me stay here."

I got on the plane totally confused. Could it be that there are actually no bad guys in Seattle? Or is it that after living in New York, my bar is set so low I don't recognize them?

Then it dawned on me: there is no douchey part of town. There is no douchebag bar. Because once you actually talk to someone, despite looking like one thing on the outside, they very rarely live up to it on the inside. We have all these ideas that maybe you can avoid a bad guy if you never date the ones who dress a certain way, have a certain type of job, have certain hobbies, or hang out at a particular bar. But that's not how it works.

Were there douchebags in Seattle? For sure. I read through the surveys (before I lost them) and found a number of them. The thing is, they weren't all congregated at one bar dressed the same way; they were scattered everywhere—in different groups of friends, wearing different types of clothes, and in totally different settings. That's the bad news: crappy guys live among us, everywhere, and they have a wide variety of disguises. The good news is: they do seem to be few and far between. Fewer and farther between than you might suspect.

Does He Want Me
or "The Chase"?

A quick note: This book is written assuming that you're looking for a relationship with the guy whose behavior you're analyzing. Not because all girls want relationships all of the time, but because you don't waste your time assessing a situation with a guy you're not that into. When a guy is nothing more than a hookup, you're probably not overly concerned about what he's thinking or feeling. During parts of this book, it may seem like guys are the ones controlling relationships. They aren't. It's just that many of the situations we're looking at are instances when you're in a vulnerable position (or at least think you are)—because again, those are usually the times you have questions. Remember, there are plenty of times you've had the upper hand and some poor guy has sat around analyzing what you're thinking.

I Want to Meet a Good Guy. Can It Happen at a Bar?

Late one Saturday over pierogies and Key lime pie, a guy friend of mine spilled his guts about his indecision over breaking up with a long-term girlfriend.

"Do you want to marry her?" I asked.

He picked at his pie silently.

"DO YOU WANT TO MARRY HER?!? Just spit it out. Just say it honestly right now, and then we can both forget this conversation ever took place."

"No . . . I don't." He looked up at me with 4 a.m. drunk eyes. "I think we would wake up in 10 years unhappy." Back to the pie, "But if I don't marry her, who do I marry? Some random girl I meet at a bar?"

Exactly. That's the fear that keeps most people in failing relationships: How do I meet someone else? It's also the thing that's the scariest about being single: looking around a bar and thinking, "I'm supposed to end up with one of you jokers?"

It's the perennial problem with meeting men: It's probably the easiest to do at a bar, but when you meet guys at bars, you're more likely to catch them with their asshole flags at full mast. Not that we really need research to back this up, but alcohol doesn't exactly turn frogs into Prince Charmings.

While collecting surveys, I kept track of where they had been filled out: a bar, a park, a fast-food spot, etc.—so I could see if where I met guys affected their answers. Sure enough, it did. Of the guys I met in bars, 56% said they'd fake an interest in a girl just to get her in bed (versus 41% of guys not in bars). And 44% of guys in bars (versus 33% of guys not in bars) said they would lie about their relationship intentions in order to sleep with a girl.

Guys in bars are more willing to lie to get themselves laid. That's not really all that surprising. But here's what is: Of *all* guys I surveyed, 73% said their primary interest in women is someone to have a long-term relationship with, and 95% said they want to get married someday. Those stats also held true for the guys I met in bars. Maybe during nights out, guys are more likely to be sexually sketchy, but their overall life goals (as far as women are concerned) aren't any different from guys you'd meet anywhere else.

It's not that guys in bars are inherently shadier than guys who don't hang out at bars (that is, that they want to lead a perpetual bachelor lifestyle). It's that once a guy walks into a bar, he's more likely to put on his douche cap. As a 27-year-old in Houston put it: "Every guy wants a relationship . . . that's the long-term goal. The short-term goal is to have a good weekend and a good story to tell." Meeting a drunk guy in "short-term" mindset doesn't guarantee he's going to be a dick, but it does increase the chances.

Another reason guys in bars may be more likely to treat you badly is because they're complete strangers. When I challenged guys about their sketchy behaviors (i.e., lying to sleep with a girl), many echoed a sentiment similar to what a guy told me in New York: "When it's just some girl you met in a bar, you don't owe her anything. It's not like she's a friend of a friend, you never have to see her again." Basically, when a guy doesn't know you, he may feel less of an incentive to look out for your needs because he doesn't have to be held accountable for his behavior.

So what does all this mean? Should you be completely unwilling to meet a guy in a bar? I don't think so—as long as you're okay with the occasional drinker. What it means is that if you're looking for a boyfriend, you have to be smart about how you go about pursuing things after you've met. Take the boy out of the bar! And no, I don't mean take him home with you.

If you meet a guy at your local watering hole, your best move is to exchange numbers and then make plans to meet up again when he's in a more wholesome frame of mind and can clearly evaluate his choices. That way, you have a chance to actually get to know each other. The better he knows you, the less likely he is to act irresponsibly because you become a real person, not just "some girl he met in a bar." And the better you know him, the more accurately *you* can judge if he's the type of guy you would want to go home with in the first place.

The problem with sleeping with a drunk guy you've just met is that he may not actually be interested in dating you. *But* he might still act interested because he's drunk, not functioning with a full deck, and "owes you nothing" (since you're basically a stranger). A guy in Boston gave this explanation for how he ends up in one-night stands with girls he's not actually that interested in: "There's drunk Sam, and then there's sober Sam. Sober Sam hates drunk Sam." Drinking can make people selfish, gluttonous, and immoral, and when you mix sex into that equation it's not likely to yield a positive result.

More about this in the Sex and Dating chapter (pages 117–139), but another potential problem with sleeping with a guy you've just met is that it might mess up the chances of starting something serious with him. And if you see potential there, why risk putting yourself in the category of "things drunk Sam did"? It doesn't matter how great you are; if a guy only vaguely remembers talking to you when he was hammered, the next morning how is he supposed to know if he should try to date you or run—as quickly as possible—away from his drunk mistake?

Guys in bars can act like assholes. That has another implication on your dating life too. This may seem a bit counterintuitive, but I'd say not to immediately dismiss a guy who hits on you at a bar. If you're not into him at all, that's one thing. But if he seems like he might be decent (before his friend bought three rounds of Patrón), maybe give him a chance to prove himself by the light of day, when his fangs shrink and his fur coat goes away. How many great guys do you know who have completely blown it with a girl because they were drunk and acted like an idiot? I can say my Key-lime-pie friend is guilty of this on many occasions. It can be hard to meet people. I'm a huge proponent of seeing every opportunity through (and by "opportunity" I don't mean guys who are definite no's, I mean the ones who are solid maybes).

You *can* meet decent guys at bars. But that doesn't mean that bars are the only places you should be trying to meet them. You can meet guys pretty much anywhere. Trust me on this one; I've been stalking them all over the country.

On a recent flight I was seated next to a 24-year-old investment banker who was bummed about not having enough battery power on his laptop to do work. Lucky for him, I was fully charged, so he got a four-hour interrogation about his dating preferences. After agreeing to answer some questions, I pulled up the document with my list. Of course, the first question on the page—in bold letters—was "Are you open to girls hitting on you anywhere? Or just in bars?"

I'd gotten used to looking sketchy, but this interaction really took the cake. "I'm not hitting on you right now, I promise, this is actually something I'm curious about for my book."

I don't think he fully believed me, but he did answer anyway: "Yes, absolutely . . . I would love for a girl to hit on me anywhere; that would be great! In a way it even feels more authentic when a girl approaches you somewhere other than a bar. At a bar it can feel like 'let's find the lowest common denominator of what we can take home.' It can feel forced. If a girl took that same approach in, like, a supermarket or something . . . it just feels more genuine. And if you have to think back about where you met your future wife, you don't want it to be in a blackout bar. Even if there's not a good story attached to it, you at least don't want it to have happened at a place you're ashamed you were at."

If you want to improve your chances of meeting someone, you have to be okay with talking to guys anywhere. In a grocery store ("whatcha plan on doing with all that mac and cheese?"), in a Best Buy ("that's a lotta inches of screen you're looking at"), on your lunch break ("you think turkey and Swiss is the way to go here?"), or any other place you see them. The more open you are to meeting people, the more guys you'll meet, and the more likely you are to find one who's worth your while.

Can I Make the First Move, or Will He Think I'm Desperate?

Four o'clock on a Friday in Seattle, and I hadn't slept well in three days. The friend I was staying with had an air mattress that deflated at least once a night, and two schizophrenic cats that ran over my face in between deflations. My plan had been to survey the happy hour crowd, but it was hot, I was tired, and the first bar I went to just didn't have enough potential targets. So I took a seat with three dudes in hipster sunglasses. They were tattooed enough to suggest they were in a punk band in high school, but had enough virgin skin to indicate that phase of their life had ended.

One of them poured me a beer from their pitcher and told me about "the Seattle Freeze"—the idea that it's impossible to meet a boyfriend or girlfriend in Seattle.

"I'm a bartender and I see it all the time. No one, girls or guys, is very approachable. People want something perfect, but they want it to fall in their laps; they aren't willing to go out and look for it. When people go out, they stick to their clique instead of meeting new people."

Now, maybe Seattleites are particularly icy, but I think to some extent this holds true everywhere. Cities are full of lonely people dying to connect with someone, but at the same time unwilling to start a conversation, and too scared to ask each other out (unless they're hammered at a pickup bar).

As girls, we get the shit end of the stick too, because we've been told that guys are the ones who are supposed to approach first, and that we have to wait for them to ask us out. We have this deeply ingrained belief that making a move on a guy would somehow disrupt the natural order of things. And this myth is made worse by poorly thought out self-help books claiming that asking a guy out is too aggressive, will scare him off, looks desperate, or ruins "the hunt." Or, that if he was "that into you" he'd reach deep into his boxer briefs, find his balls, and mosey on over and say hello.

But that's all crap. Half of the guys I surveyed said that a girl asking them out is a turn-on. Nearly everyone else (45%) said they didn't care either way, and only 5% said it was too aggressive.

A girl who knows what she wants and goes after it is hot— that's something I heard again and again. According to a guy I met in DC: "Confidence can bump a 6 up to an 8, and lack of it can bring a 9 down to a 7." In a survey question, I asked guys to rank a handful of traits they might look for in a girlfriend, and then asked them to write in any other characteristics they thought were important. The most common write-in answer: confidence.

You can—and should—ask guys out. More than the fact that it shows self-assurance, guys are just sick of doing all the work. For many, approaching a girl and asking her out is scary as hell because, as one Los Angeles guy expressed: "If you're not doing well with girls, who are you? You're worthless."

I caught a 23-year-old finance guy in Chicago having a late lunch and eager to complain about how much it sucks to be a guy and be expected to make all the effort. "The main reason I don't approach girls is because it's awkward—I may get rejected, and then it takes down my day. It seems like girls these days are lacking personality. They expect guys to do everything! They should approach us more, and ask us out!" He paused and took out his frustration by aggressively tearing into a bag of potato chips, first with his hands, then with his mouth. "Be original, you know? Ask me to see a chick flick! I won't say no! Some are kinda funny!"

And there you have it. The money shot. Carte blanche to ask a guy to the next Jennifer Aniston/Lopez/Garner flick that hits theaters.

The point here is, many guys would be psyched to have a girl ask them out on a date. So psyched, that they're happy to do anything once they're on it. You really can't go wrong.

It's a similar sentiment to one expressed when I was interviewing guys for an article about the "best ways to pick up a man." The article was nearly impossible to write because most guys couldn't get past the excitement of a girl making the effort to talk to them. "What works best? I don't know, 'Hi,' 'Hello,' burp in my face . . . I mean, pretty much anything."

Guys appreciate when you make the first move, and no, it doesn't ruin "the hunt." I wouldn't smack a dude in the face and go, "Yeah, bitch! You like that? Meet me for dinner tomorrow!" But honestly, even doing that might end up okay. A good-looking 26-year-old grad student told me this: "I don't think guys enjoy the hunt as much as girls enjoy being hunted. Most guys just want to find the right person without having to put themselves out there constantly. I'm someone who is very outgoing and relatively unafraid to walk up and start talking to a group of girls. But even for those of us on the braver side, it's not easy to approach a group of strangers who will instantly judge us for the first few things we do or say. We all have degrees of self-doubt. It would be nice to not be the one who has to walk up to a new group of girls, but rather have them approach us."

If you were to ask a guy out (according to my survey results, anyway), there's a 50% chance he'll like you more because of it. There is a 45% chance it won't change his feelings either way, and only one guy out of 20 will feel it was a bit aggressive—though if he likes you, he'll probably go out with you anyway. In the words of one 28-year-old, "If you're into a girl, you'll make any excuse for her."

Being unwilling to approach a guy means that you never get to choose for yourself—you only get a chance with the guys who were bold enough to approach you. And really, what's the worst that could happen? He acts uninterested. Or you ask him out and he says no. And then so what? Your heart explodes out of your eyeballs? The world blows up? Life as we know it gets eradicated? No. You shrug him off, have a greater appreciation for how guys feel when you've rejected them, and move on to someone else. Being turned down (especially if it's by a stranger) just isn't that horrific. Guys' advances get blown off all the time, and they still live to tell about it. I think that we're strong enough to endure the same "suffering."

A guy once told me, "Meeting girls is 80% effort. It's not about being amazing-looking, or the coolest and most interesting guy in the bar, it's about putting yourself out there, realizing you're going to get rejected a lot, but continuing to go for it anyway." This approach works for us too. In my experience, it's the girls who aren't afraid to go for it who end up getting the most (and best) guys.

Why Did That D-Bag Ask for My Number but Never Call?

Wars may have been fought over women, but distilleries have been drained, entire regions sucked dry, over this one: Why didn't he call? Why would a guy go through the trouble of asking for a phone number and then not use it? Percentage wise, here's your answer:

"You got a girl's number and then never called, why?"

38%	
Weren't interested	
31%	
Reassessed the situation	
5%	
Got the number out of obligation	
5%	
Plain wussed out	
5%	
Were too busy	
4%	
Got the number for fun/an ego boost	
12%	
Gave some other excuse	

0%   100%

It's worth mentioning that 13% of guys who filled out the survey said they would never do this—that if they got a girl's number they would always call. As for the rest of them, here's some elaboration:

"Not interested/Not *that* interested." A little over a third of guys said they didn't call because they weren't interested. The question is: If they weren't interested, why did they get the number in the first place? The best insight I have came from a 27-year-old

PALM BEACH COUNTY
LIBRARY SYSTEM
Library name: WBOYNTON
561-734-5556
Checkout Date: 03/02/2021

Title: Are All Guys Assholes? :
More Than 1,000 Guys...
Call Number: 306.73 MAD
Item ID: R0061476651
Date Due: 3/23/2021

Check your account at:
http://www.pbclibrary.org

from New Mexico (who I met in Houston): "It's better to have a girl's number and not need it than to need a girl's number and not have it." Basically, they got your number to keep their options open.

Annoying yes, but if we're honest, we do this too. Haven't you given your number to a guy because you figure "Why not?" And maybe you're not *really* interested, but decide you'll delay making the final judgment—like shoving a shirt you haven't worn in two years back into the drawer "just in case." It's selfish, but natural, to be a bit indecisive when it comes to dating.

Some guys in this group said specifically that they weren't *that* interested. Yes, the dreaded "that." What does *that* mean? *That* is the fact that calling someone you don't know can be awkward. That planning a date is both time-consuming and expensive. That arranging to meet up even casually requires a certain amount of effort. *That* simply means that if the girl were on one side of the scale and laziness was on the other, the laziness would win. As one guy wrote, "Considered it to be too much work to call her." It's not that they weren't interested at all, it's that they weren't interested enough . . . to get off their asses and do something about it. Again, not the shiniest side of human nature, but human nonetheless.

"Reassessed the situation." Almost another third of guys didn't call because they "reassessed the situation." This means that at the time the guy got your number he really did intend to call you. But then he talked himself out of it: Was there really a connection there? Is this definitely something I want to pursue? Was there a red flag that made me question the feasibility of dating her? Do I *like* like her? In the words of one guy: "I got her number because I was excited in the moment, but wasn't excited enough later on to call her."

The most common perpetrator accused of causing false excitement was—as you might imagine—alcohol. "I was drunk." I read that answer a lot. I think it's safe to assume that drinking was also a major factor for guys who got the numbers of girls they weren't actually interested in. Perhaps they thought they might have been at the time, but when they sobered up, they changed their minds. Fair enough. It's easy to get wrapped up in the moment. Hell, I even have girls' numbers in my phone from nights out when I convinced myself I'd just met my new best friend. Natalie Awesome, Emily Awesomer, Kelly the Shit. Did I believe we were kindred spirits at the time? Absolutely. Did I ever call them? Nope.

The other problem with being drunk: You just don't remember too good. "I don't remember her name/what she looked like." That one also popped up a good number of times. If a guy doesn't remember talking to you, he's not going to call you. That's no insult to you—you just caught him at a bad time.

"Felt obligated." Some guys feel there is such an expectation for them to make a move that not asking a girl for her digits is insulting. A guy in New York told me this: "If you've spent a good amount of time talking to a girl, then it's kinda rude not to ask for her number. Sometimes I'll get a girl's number just because I feel like I'm obligated to do it, not because I'm actually interested." In the same way that we might feel pressure to give our number to a guy we've spent a while talking to (or one who has bought us a drink), guys can feel pressured to ask for it.

"Got the number for fun/ego boost." You could get pissed at the guys who answered this way, but really, it's just pathetic. These are the kind of guys who bond with their friends over "you know how I know you're gay" jokes. They're trying to show their friends how straight and macho they are by getting a bunch of girls' numbers. But they aren't actually interested in the girls; they're interested in looking good in front of the fellas—which is ironically homoerotic for guys who are trying so hard to look straight. Or, they just need the confidence boost of knowing a girl would give them the number . . . in which case, you gotta just feel bad for them. Luckily, only 4% of guys out there are actually this lame.

When a guy gets your number and doesn't call, it's annoying. But guys don't do it with the intention of upsetting you or ruining your week. I think we have to let them off the hook a bit on this one because initiating contact, planning a date, and taking a girl out—that's a lot of work (and possibly a lot of money). For better or worse, as girls, all we have to do is show up. The heavy lifting is mostly on the guy.

On a recent "personal date" (while sketchily also writing a book about dating), I lost a bet and was charged with planning the next time we went out. It was *much* tougher than I expected, and it gave me a newfound appreciation for the plight of the modern-day man. You can't go somewhere too cheap, but you don't want to go somewhere too expensive. What if it's too loud? Or too romantic and makes you both uncomfortable? Luckily, my date got sick and by the time he was better, the bet was forgotten.

As dumb as it may seem for a guy to go through the trouble of getting your number and then never actually use it, it's much better than pursuing you if he's unsure of his feelings. And though it may be a bit insulting, it's no judgment on your desirability because a guy you've just met doesn't actually know you.

If you meet a guy that you'd be heartbroken if you never heard from, instead of giving him your number, take his. Put the ball in your court: "All right, buddy, how about I get *your* number, and then I'll decide whether or not to call *you*."

Guys want to find a relationship every bit as badly as we do. But because dating traditions say that guys are supposed to be the pursuers, it creates the illusion that they have all the power, because it puts *us* in the position of waiting for *them*. They have the power to act, and we only have the option of how to respond to their actions. Guys aren't "naturally" in control of dating situations, and if you don't want to be in the position of waiting around for a call, get his number, so that you can be the one to hold the reins.

We Hit It Off Great. Why Did He Wait Three Days to Call? And What Does That Mean?

When a guy gets your number, you're not going to hear from him for at least a few days. Unless of course, he's trying to play it Rico Suave, in which case he'll text something cute that night that probably includes your name. That's not a statistic I picked up officially, just after years of experience talking to guys, and knowing when they think they're being seductive. That's right, buddy, I took Intro to Psychology in college too—I know I like hearing my own name.

If we can talk in averages, expect to hear from a guy in two to four days. It's the three-day rule. As a guy in Houston explained: "You have to wait three days. If you don't, then she has the cards because you liked her so much you couldn't wait. Or you had nothing better to do than call her. If you wait, it gives her some doubt, and makes her want you more."

Many, many guys I spoke with subscribed to this rule. Which is pretty funny because it's not like it's some closely guarded secret of the male community; it's something most people know about. Meaning, any "good" it might do probably gets negated since it's so transparent. And yet, many guys still swear it's the secret ingredient to their dating successes.

The funny thing is, even guys who don't wait simply for the sake of waiting can end up waiting about three days. When I gave a guy in Atlanta crap about the "three-day rule" he retorted with this: "Look, it just takes that long to get yourself together. Assuming you met a girl on the weekend, you go back to work, get on top of your week, and by Tuesday or Wednesday you're ready to start planning a date."

Speaking in averages again, your guy is going to see if you want to get "a drink after work" sometime during the week. No first dates on weekends. That's another rule many of the guys I spoke with subscribed to. It's a combination of not wanting to give up their weekends, not wanting to look like they didn't have anything better to do on their weekends, and not wanting to come on too strong by asking you to give up yours. A 23-year-old told me: "You ask to see a girl during the week because you want to act like your weekends are planned out."

"Well, are they?" I asked.

"No . . . but . . . I don't know . . . on the weekends is when you want to hang out with your friends."

Other guys asked for weekday dates not because they wanted to seem like they had such busy schedules, but because they wanted to increase the likelihood of fitting into yours. One guy said, "Girls are more likely to be busy during the weekend. So they're more likely to say yes to a date on a Wednesday or Thursday."

Of course, not all guys play by these rules. In general, the older guys I talked to seemed less interested in playing games and jumping through hoops. One 35-year-old software developer said, "In your 30s, you just don't give a shit about the little things you gave a shit about in your 20s. When I was younger, I thought that's just what people in their 30s said to make themselves feel better. But now that I'm older, I get it." There are plenty of guys, of all ages, who shoot from the hip and call you whenever it makes sense in their schedule, which would obviously vary from week to week and girl to girl.

Long story short: Whenever you hear from a guy, it's a sign he's interested. It's not worth your time trying to find meaning in *when* he contacted you, because so many guys wait a few days no matter what, just to try to keep you on your toes. The fact that it may have taken him some time to get in touch means absolutely nothing about how much he likes you.

One situation where you might want to raise your eyebrows is this: You meet a guy at a bar and don't hear from him again until the next weekend when he's out. In this case, you may have met a guy who's just looking for a booty call.

The other possibility is that you've met a guy who's just not a dater. I talked to many guys who preferred to see a girl they've just met in a more casual setting rather than a high-pressure "date." In that case, a very well-intentioned guy may be inviting you to meet up with his friends at a bar. One guy told me: "I'm not going to get in touch with a girl unless I'm doing something fun I can invite her to." And for a guy who goes with the flow and doesn't make plans until the last minute, that may very well mean he's texting you when he's out the next weekend. As a guy from Denver wrote: "Like most guys, I don't make plans. Rather, I have a vague idea of what I feel like doing and determine the details less than a day in advance."

If it's 11 p.m. on a Friday and a guy who's likely had a few drinks is trying to meet up with you, either he's just looking to hook up, he doesn't like "dating," or he's a bad planner (or perhaps he was too scared to get in touch when he was sober). There's no way of knowing which one of these is true unless you get to know him better. If you're worried that he's just looking for a hookup and that's not what you're into, then meet up with him, *don't* hook up with him, and give him another chance to get in touch when he's sober.

Is He Texting Because He Wants to Put Forth as Little Effort as Possible?

Don't be surprised if the first time a guy asks you out it's through a text message. And this has less to do with his laziness, and more to do with his not wanting to screw things up. A 32-year-old New Yorker said: "I just sound so much wittier over text. It's not that I don't want to put forth the effort to call, I just want to put my best foot forward." That 30-second delay really does wonders for a man's bantering ability, as well as his ability to not sound like a complete and total bonehead. A 26-year-old told me: "With a text, you get to think about what you want to say, proofread it twice, and then send it."

In the original survey I asked guys about their favorite method of communicating with a girl they liked. Their options were: Facebook, texting, calling, e-mailing, and other. While 34% of guys said they prefer to talk to a girl via text, 46% said they prefer to talk to a girl on the phone. A full 15% checked "other," and wrote in "in person"—a sign of the times that I completely neglected to give that as an option.

I decided to write a follow-up survey after realizing that a few of the questions (like this one) didn't give enough answer choices, and discovering that there were some topics I just needed to explore further. I distributed that survey online and it was answered by 200 guys (in the same demographic as the first one: unmarried, ages 22–45, heterosexual). In this online survey, I asked guys about their preferred method of talking to a girl and included "in-person" as a choice. Given this option, 65% of guys chose in-person communication as their preferred method (17% said texting, and only 10% said calling). It turns out, guys want to talk with you in the flesh rather than blow up your phone. As a 24-year-old said to me: "I don't call a girl I've just started dating because I don't want to get to know her over the phone; I want to get to know her in person. So texts are just logistical. It's easier to coordinate over text messages."

If you've gone on a few dates with a guy and never had a long phone chat, I wouldn't read anything into it: Some guys just don't like talking on the phone. A 28-year-old revealed he can't stand the phone, because he "never knows how to end the conversation, and always feels guilty about hanging up." Seems like a strange fear to me, but hey, we all have our own neuroses.

A guy texting you instead of calling has nothing to do with how much he likes you, how much effort he's willing to put into the relationship, or how good of a guy he is. (Although if the guy seems hilarious over text and in person can't string an interesting/intelligent sentence together, then I might worry you've caught yourself a dud . . . though perhaps a dud with a really funny roommate.)

The only reason to worry is if your relationship is all texting. No talking on the phone, no meeting up in person—so no *actual* conversations. The thing about texting is that it requires virtually no effort. A question on my survey asked guys why they would continue to text a girl but make no effort to actually meet up with her. Many answers were something to the tune of "texting is just too easy." A relationship that is all texting is not a relationship. A few texts here and there with no other efforts to talk or hang out is a sure sign of a guy trying to string you along, rather than one having genuine interest.

CASE STUDY: KURT

I met Kurt when he was 26, and it was his last week in New York before moving to the Midwest for business school. He's now 28, and I've followed his dating life for more than a year and a half with regular phone calls about the girls entering and exiting his life.

I have all of our conversations written down in a notebook. About a third of the way in at the top of a page is this quote, "I'm getting pretty ready to find someone. My biological clock is definitely ticking, and I know that I'd be happier at work if I had a family." And then at the bottom of that same page (something he must have said two minutes later): "I also had fun hooking up with undergraduates last year." I'd say that pretty much sums it up. Kurt would be ready to settle down if he met the right girl, but he's not so mature that he wouldn't have flings with much-younger girls he would never actually consider dating. And in that sense, he made the perfect case study. A guy capable of both good and bad choices—sliding somewhere between prince and asshole, depending on the situation. So it's illuminating to know, which situations brought out the prince?

In the year and a half that we've been talking, he's had a good number of hookups, gone on quite a few dates, and had two girl-friends. Looking back over his experiences, both of the girls he ended up seriously dating were ones he viewed very differently from those he just hooked up with. He described the girls with whom he got serious as "independent" and "the type who don't take any crap." When I asked why he found these traits attractive, he answered, "You want someone who knows what they want, and knows they're worth getting it." He later elaborated in an e-mail:

"Basically, you want the girl you end up with to be a catch. That doesn't necessarily mean the hottest girl, or the biggest party girl, or the smartest girl. I think what that means to me is someone that picks you as much as you pick them. I know that I want a strong girl—and with that, I like the thought that she sees something in me that she doesn't just find anywhere else. That may be part of the male 'ego' with courtship—who knows.

"I think what turns me off—and a lot of guys—are the girls who just want to be in a relationship because that's where they get their self-esteem from. Implicit in that is that in some senses, the guys they are with are just interchangeable. How do girls give off that sense? Basically, by not realizing that the guy is lucky to be with them. When they let themselves get walked on, they give off the vibe they're desperate for a guy—*any* guy—just because they need to fill that void."

A guy you're dating or hooking up with wants you to stand up for yourself. If he's not treating you well, or giving you the type of relationship you want, he wants you to call him on it. Guys need to know you're not so desperate for a male presence in your life that you're willing to lower your standards for how you should be treated. Not only does that insult you, it insults him. Because if you're so desperate for *a guy*, it shows you'd take any guy. And that means the guy you're involved with just isn't that special.

San Francisco: Same Shit, Different Day

It was early evening in the Marina in San Francisco, and I was waiting for the happy hour crowd to get going. I stumbled upon the original Benefit cosmetics store and decided to take a little break and get my makeup done. Whenever I come out of one of those places I look like a train wreck, but for some reason I still find it relaxing. I had a cold, was exhausted, and just felt like getting pampered. "All right, ladies, show me what you got."

As the saleslady dusted me in makeup I would never wear and had no intention of buying, we made small talk and I told her why I was in town.

"You know," she said, "I see the same girls in here every weekend getting their makeup done before they go out to a club. And every week they're bitching about this guy or that guy. Some weeks they come in really upset and can barely stop crying long enough for me to do their eyes. But they're in here week after week, getting done up for the same clubs, meeting the same guys. And I keep wondering, why are they still hanging out with the same shitty guys?"

Good question. It's one thing to get screwed over by a guy. But it's another to get screwed over again and again by the same guy. Or to continue to put yourself in the same situations where you've ended up unhappy the next day. *Get a new plan.*

Yes, it's easier to just blame guys for acting badly, but if a situation is making you unhappy, it's *your* responsibility to get out of it. If you keep meeting the same lame guys every weekend, scoop up your friends and try another part of town or another type of bar. If your track record with the guys you meet at bars doesn't look so hot, start meeting them elsewhere. If you've been hooking up with the same guy for months and he always makes you feel like crap, stop talking to him. If your boyfriend is a complete loser who takes you for granted, don't just bitch about him—dump him.

You can only blame guys up to a point. Eventually you have to decide to stop repeating your past mistakes. Take the responsibility to look out for your own well-being. Because in the words of former president George W. Bush, "Fool me once, shame on you. Fool me—you can't get fooled *again*!"

Does He Think
I'm a Stage-Five Clinger
Because I Texted Him?

DATING

Is Looking Hot the Most Important Thing in Terms of Getting a Guy?

If you're like most girls, there's probably at least a part of you that thinks the best way to get a guy is to look hot. Or that maybe if you lost five pounds or had cuter clothes, you'd be luckier in love. We're not crazy or insanely vain for thinking this way, it's the crap we're spoon-fed from the second we open our eyes. From Disney (the *beautiful* princess gets the prince) to *Maxim* (hottest hotties stripping down!), we're constantly told how important it is to look good. And we hear this so much that it's easy to start believing our value to men is completely wrapped up in our physical attractiveness.

From a financial standpoint, this is an important belief to per-petuate, because it's how companies sell us shit. Sexy Face mascara: "Give yourself lashes longer than the hard-on he gets when he sees you wearing it!" New diet book: "You're single because you eat too many carbs." By waving the promise of men's affection, brands try to keep us obsessed with our looks, because what would happen if women collectively decided they no longer cared? The fash-ion industry, diet industry, plastic surgery industry, spa industry, beauty and skin-care industry, many women's magazines—they'd all tank. I mean, we'd be looking at another global financial cri-sis. So as many marketing campaigns may suggest that being just a little cuter is the key to romantic success, that's just not the case.

When assessing initiatives in public health, they talk about failed effort versus failed strategy. Failed effort in this case would mean not having spent enough time at the gym and neglecting to buy the latest lip-plumping gloss. Failed strategy is spending all of your time thinking about what you look like, and not making an effort to be funny or interesting to talk to (or being so hungry because of your latest diet that you're acting like a total bitch).

Relying on your looks as the primary way to attract and keep a guy does not work! And it's not because of failed effort (that you don't *quite* look good enough)—it's because of failed strategy. This isn't just my opinion; I heard it constantly from all types of guys.

"These girls get all dolled up to go out, but then you talk to them and they have their nose in the air and no personality. They need to let down their guard and show who they are."—28-year-old hipster in San Francisco

"It's all about the conversation. If the conversation goes flat, forget it. You can find lots of good-looking girls—you need one you can talk to."—preppy 26-year-old in New York

"I don't care how hot she is; if she has a lack of intellect and individuality, then forget it."—26-year-old geeky-cute programmer in Atlanta

Not only do guys care about things other than a girl's looks, they care about those other things more. I asked guys to rate how important various traits were in a girlfriend on a scale from 1 (not important) to 5 (very important). Here's the breakdown of what percentage of guys gave each trait a 5.

Another way to look at guys' answers is through averages. This is how each trait netted out overall.

Average score guys gave each trait

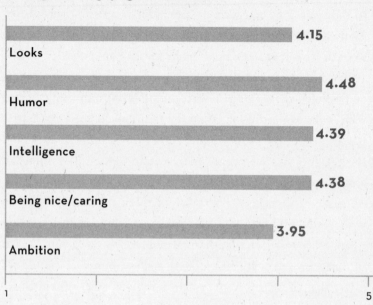

Counter to what *Maxim* would have you believe, guys aren't actually that shallow. Turns out, they think with their brains, not just their dicks. No matter which way you slice it, guys care about much more than good looks. And they consistently rank looks as less important than being sweet, smart, and funny. Are looks important? Yes. All of these traits were. But they are by no means the be-all and end-all of what guys are looking for in a girl.

Here's the thing: There are millions of pretty girls in the world. So if all you are is a pretty face on a cute body, you're completely disposable. Yes, you will get guys' attention initially, but will they stick around? No. So take showers, smell good, stay well groomed, dress for your body, eat for your blood type, blah-blah-blah. But know that aside from the prerequisite looking decent, if you want to interest a guy, you have to show him you have a personality. Don't act like an airhead, don't be a bitch, throw him a bone and smile at his jokes, and dare to make some of your own.

If you're a career-oriented girl, you may look at these results and wonder what's going on with ambition (the only trait that tied with looks for last place). We've all heard about the Best Actress Oscar curse. Reese Witherspoon, Halle Berry, Sandra Bullock (and the list goes on) all got divorced within a year of winning an Oscar—presumably indicating that career success is harmful to romantic relationships. (Personally, I think this has more to do with Hollywood being bad for romantic relationships. I'm sure many other actresses who didn't win anything got divorced each of those years as well.) But looking at these numbers, should we worry that guys don't want to date ambitious, successful girls?

No, not at all. First of all, it's not like guys were consistently ranking ambition with ones and twos. An average score of 3.95 still means they find ambition important. What these numbers do indicate is that guys want someone ambitious, but first and foremost they want a companion more than they want a provider. And, much like puppy dogs, they want your attention. A lawyer I met in Boston told me this: "At first when a girl is really into her career, it's a turn-on. But then you start dating her, realize that means she has less time for you, and that's tough."

On the other hand, there are also guys who live and die by their careers, whose jobs are their passion as well as their profession. Those types of guys think it's very important to find a girl who's just as driven and energized by her career. A 24-year-old financial analyst who works about 80 hours a week told me: "I couldn't imagine ending up with a girl who stayed home and didn't have her own career that she was passionate about. I'd get so bored with someone like that."

All in all, guys want to be with a girl who is well rounded. Not just a pretty face or a go-getter, but someone who they can talk to, laugh with, and feel comforted by.

Before a First Date, I'm Freaking Out. Are Guys Scared at All?

Waiting outside a bar one night, I got into a conversation with the bouncer about dates. "Dates are stupid. In no other real-life scenario would you be sitting across a table from someone, completely removed from your normal surroundings, and trying to decide if you're compatible or not. That's not how you should get to know someone, because you're probably not getting to know them that well. To get to know someone you have to do things with them, hang out with their friends, and invite them to hang out with yours. Get a sense of how they fit into your life, not just how they are in one—completely bizarre—situation."

Dating can be rough. It's like going on a job interview where sexual harassment is okay. There's a reason that many dates involve alcohol: If you like the guy, they're freaking scary . . . and if you don't, they're just painful. Like I said, a reason many involve alcohol.

But how do guys feel about dating? (Aside from that bouncer who clearly is not a fan.) Do they stress out about it? Do they get nervous?

For the most part, yes. Just like us, guys are a little freaked out before a date. But the extent varies. A few guys told me they get so nervous that they show up at the bar/restaurant a half hour early and take shots. Others told me dates were "fun" and said they don't get very nervous at all. Most guys I spoke with said their level of nervousness really depended on how much they liked the girl.

On the original survey I asked guys to rate their first date nervousness on a scale from 1 to 10, with 1 being "not scared at all," and 10 being "shitting in your pants." On average, guys rated their nervousness at a 4. (One guy actually added that he shits his pants at least once a year "to maintain a humble outlook on life," but that's neither here nor there.) Here is the actual distribution:

"Before a first date, how nervous are you on a scale from 1 to 10?"

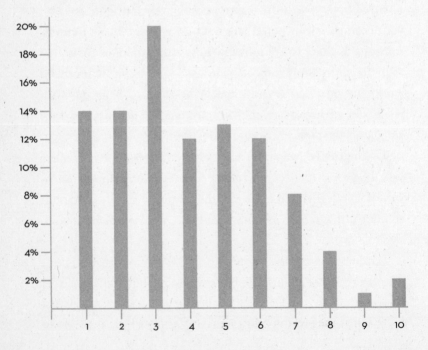

On average, I think it's safe to assume that on a first date a guy has a good amount of butterflies. He's on edge about impressing you, but can probably hold it together enough to look at least semi-normal. This means two things. One: Cut him some slack. Try not to be too judgmental, because nerves don't bring out the best in anyone. If he's a complete ass, be judgmental. But if he's slightly awkward, reaching a bit for conversation topics, or asking you some kinda lame questions, try to withhold judgment until he warms up a little.

Two: Relax. It's okay to be nervous on a date. Guys are nervous too. They want it to go well just as much as you do. (Remember that nearly three-quarters of *all* guys are primarily interested in women because they want to find a long-term relationship—and it's probably safe to assume that percentage is much higher among guys who are taking girls on dates). Guys may act overly confident, but nervousness is a guy emotion every bit as much as a girl one. And yes, they get nervous about romantic situations, not just football scores.

Sometimes it helps walking into a date knowing a guy is having the same butterflies that you are. And if you really can't control your nerves . . . just think about him crapping his pants. Nothing brings down someone's intimidation factor like imagining them on the crapper (or in this case, not quite reaching it).

Did He Not Kiss Me Because He Doesn't Like Me?

On a Wednesday night you go to a bar to have a few drinks with a guy you met the previous weekend. At first it's awkward . . . you're peeling the label off your beer, shredding the coaster, and he's getting a sweaty brow. But you push through, order another drink, and things start to feel more normal. He tells some stories that aren't actually that interesting, but you listen to them intently, and act like you care. By the end of the night, you guys are both laughing and getting along really well. He pays and you walk outside.

"Thanks so much," you say, swinging your bag, biting your lip, trying to look cute.

"Yup." He gives you a dude-bro nod. "It was fun hanging out." Pause. "Weeeeeell . . . have a good rest of your week." And with that, the date is over.

WTF? No kiss? That can't be good, right? Rest of your week . . . what does that mean? Is it a bad sign? Does he think you're just friends? Wait, was this even a date . . .

We've had it pounded into our skulls that guys are supposed to jump at any possible opportunity to get it on—so when a guy isn't trying to shove his tongue down your throat at the end of a date, it can feel oddly alarming. But if the date went well, don't freak out that he didn't kiss you. Not kissing you isn't necessarily (or even that likely) a sign of disinterest. Only 19% of guys I surveyed said that they didn't kiss a girl at the end of a date because they didn't like her very much. That means that four times out of five, it has to do with something else entirely.

About a third of guys (34%) said they didn't kiss a girl after a first date because they thought it might be too forward. Another 21% said they didn't go in for a kiss because they didn't have the opportunity, and 12% said it's because they wussed out. Finally, 14% of guys gave other reasons: They never kiss on first dates, they're taking it slow, they didn't get the vibe that it would be appropriate, or they're holding out to make you like them more (probably the result of reading some pickup book suggesting this is how to manipulate your feelings).

When a date doesn't end in a kiss, there may be no way of knowing why. But way more often than not, it's not because the guy didn't like you. It's very likely, as one 25-year-old put it, that he's just "not sure if a kiss [was] the right thing to do." So if you're going to analyze something about the date, analyze whether or not you want to see him again. Think about how interested you were in what he was saying, if he seemed full of himself, immature, or just plain sketchy. But don't waste your time worrying about the kiss. If it's meant to be, it will happen eventually.

What Happened on the Date That Turned Him Off?

We know what guys want in a girl: someone smart, fun, sweet, and attractive. But what do they *not* want? What are the dating faux pas that suck guys into that black hole, never to be heard from again? I'll give you a hint: It's not that you weren't cute enough, didn't give him an over-the-pants hand job, or weren't wearing your "sexy jeans." The reasons guys gave for losing a girl's number after a date weren't very different from the reasons we might lose a guy's. Grouped roughly into a few major categories, here are guys' biggest dating complaints:

Bad Conversation. What do guys define as bad conversation? When a girl talks too much, too little, or talks about things that are "stupid." On the "too little" side, guys complained about being

"What things turn you off most on a date?"

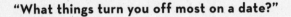

20%
Bad conversation

7%
TMI

7%
A girl who only talks about herself

16%
Bad manners

35%
Bad personality/attitude

14%
Other

0%   100%

on a date with a girl who sat there, didn't say much, had no opinion on anything, didn't make eye contact, or didn't seem to be paying attention. A guy in LA told me about a date he went on where the girl was staring at the TV behind him the entire time. He assumed she wasn't into him because she wasn't making any effort to ask questions and didn't seem that interested in what he was saying. He was shocked when she reached out to him for a second date, and unsurprisingly, he had no interest in going.

On the flip side, guys also didn't like when a girl talked too much. One 33-year-old explained it this way: "You don't want a girl who over-dominates the conversation. It should be like a tennis match." Some guys also complained about girls who talked about superficial things like the weather, money, shopping, social drama, or "things of no substance." Many wrote about wanting to be with a girl who "has a sense of what's going on in the world."

Bad conversation is a huge turnoff to many guys because (fairly or not) that's what they're using to judge who you are. The things you talk about on a date are your chance to tell a guy about your passions, your interests, your life goals, and generally what makes you tick. And of course, it's also your opportunity to get to know all those things about him.

TMI. If during a date you're at a loss for something to say, saying nothing at all is better than talking about an ex. Guys complained about this repeatedly. A guy in New York said: "If a girl is talking about her ex, it's a sign to me that she's not over him, so then why are we on a date?" Seriously, guys don't want to hear about him. No matter what. It doesn't matter how funny the story is, or how relevant it is to the conversation. All past hookups are also out. Basically, if it's about another guy, leave it alone.

Something else guys mentioned not wanting to hear about on a date (though not nearly as often as "other dudes") were your deepest, darkest, emotional scars. One 27-year-old wrote that he didn't want a girl to be "talking about all her problems, everything in her life that's going wrong, or how much she dislikes her friends." Understandably, a guy wants to feel like your date, not your therapist.

Many guys also wrote that disparaging comments about your age or weight should be off-limits. A guy I met in Brooklyn told me: "When I was 26, I went on a few dates with a woman who was 30. I didn't care about our age difference at all, but she couldn't let it go. She brought it up so much that I found her annoying and stopped wanting to see her—not because *I* cared about her age, but because *she* did."

Talking About Yourself Too Much. Some people's reaction to being nervous is to clam up and say nothing (hence, TV-watching girl). Others' reaction is to talk nonstop. And when you're talking nonstop, it's usually about yourself. "Not asking me questions about myself" was listed as a turnoff by many guys—ranging from an organic farmer to a doctor to an administrative assistant. One guy phrased this turnoff as "a girl who starts every sentence with 'I.'" Guys want to get to know you on a date, but they also want to know that you're interested in getting to know them. So be sure to ask questions about their life, their job, their family, where they grew up, etc.

The one caution guys gave about asking questions is to be sure they don't come across as thinly veiled attempts to figure out how much money a guy makes. A 28-year-old from Houston said he wanted girls to ask questions that got at "who you are, instead of just what you do. When the first question a girl asks is 'so what do you do?' it feels like she's asking, 'how much money do you have?'"

Bad Manners. We don't usually think of men as the most civilized things on the planet, but many are turned off when they go on a date with a girl who has bad manners. The three offenses guys listed most often: using your cell phone, expecting the guy to pay, and being rude. Cell phone use was the bad manner that irked the most guys. As a 27-year-old producer said: "When a girl whips out her phone on a date and starts texting a friend or checking her messages, it's like, 'Jesus, how boring am I?'" Seemingly obvious, but guys don't want to be on a date with a girl who's preoccupied with other things, or would rather be talking to someone else.

Next order of business: Who pays? One guy wrote that he was turned off by "a girl who expects me to pay—though I will," and many others complained about girls who didn't offer, or didn't say thank you. Most likely, a guy will end up paying the first time you go out, but many guys appreciate when you offer to at least split it.

The third offense guys mentioned in the manners category was being rude to others. The "others" were in most cases the waitstaff. One explained it this way: "When a girl is rude to the server, it shows she's selfish, stuck up, has no grasp on reality, and is just a spoiled brat."

Bad Personality/Attitude. This complaint is a somewhat subjective one because the definition of a "bad" attitude or personality is going to vary from guy to guy. That being said, the winners in this category were: bragging, being materialistic, having no sense of humor, and being dumb. That's right, bragging. I have to say I was pretty shocked to keep reading that over and over. But many guys complained about girls who, as one wrote, "talk nonstop about how great they are." Confidence is good, but going overboard into the territories of arrogance and self-absorption is a definite turnoff.

Coming across as materialistic pretty much speaks for itself. Quite a few guys wrote about the plight of "being treated like a checkbook instead of a person." If this is an insecurity guys have (that you don't want them, only their money), it's understandable that any sign a girl is materialistic (a few mentioned "brand dropping") would raise their eyebrows.

Guys also made clear, once again, that they want to be with a girl who is both smart and funny. A 22-year-old said: "I've learned the hard way that looks are not everything. Being able to really talk to a girl and enjoy her company are so much more important in terms of a relationship."

In case you're curious about the laundry list of other negative personality traits that at least a few guys mentioned on their surveys, here you go: being stuck up, name dropping, being judgmental, being negative, insincerity, complaining, superficiality, a girl who comes off as entitled, being too aggressive, being mean-spirited, not having fun, and finally, not smiling.

Other. Very few guys mentioned being turned off by something physical on a date. But when they did, it almost always had to do with your mouth. Guys mentioned bad breath, having dirty teeth, chewing with your mouth open, and basically anything that would hint at bad oral hygiene. Ironically, with all of the time and energy we may put into our outfit, hair, and makeup before a date, probably our most worthwhile beauty investments are a toothbrush, toothpaste, floss, and mouthwash. And if you really want to impress him, spring for some Crest Whitestrips and chew with your mouth closed. Aside from bad oral hygiene, the additional complaints that made up the "other" category were smoking, getting too drunk, and general incompatibilities.

No one wants to get rejected, so it's always at least a little disappointing when a guy doesn't call you after a date (even if in truth you didn't like him that much either). But remember, a guy isn't rejecting you; he's rejecting the snap judgment he made of you. Think back to the first impressions you had of some people you know.

Likely, who you thought they were after knowing them for a couple of hours was very different from who they turned out to be once you got to know them better. Dating is a flawed system for many reasons, but perhaps the biggest problem is that it forces people to make decisions based on relatively little information. So while it may be annoying not to get called back after a date, it's not a dis of who you *actually* are, only of the first impression you gave someone.

How Long After Our Date Is This Dick Going to Wait to Call Me?

Hey, I have a novel idea: Why don't I take a girl on a date, and then no matter what happens, wait two to three days to get in touch with her again. Yes, the three-day rule strikes again (two-thirds of the time, anyway).

To be fair, while some guys wait just to wait, others get back in touch when they can or when it feels appropriate, and that might vary by situation. One guy in Seattle wrote: "It depends what day we went out, what else I have going on that week, and maybe even how much I like her." Of course, without knowing a guy, you can't judge how much he likes you based on when he calls—since, for some guys, liking you a lot means he'll contact you sooner, and for others it means he'll wait longer in order to look like he's busy, important, and generally not desperate.

No matter what his logic (or lack thereof), 9 times out of 10, you'll hear from a guy within three days of going out with him. I asked, "How long do you usually wait to call a girl after a first date?" 27% of guys usually wait only one day, 41% wait two days, and

23% wait three. Only 7% of guys wait about a week, and 2% wait more than a week.

If you want to talk to a guy and you haven't heard from him, there's no reason you can't be the one to reach out. You don't have to wait around to hear from a guy. The only benefit of letting him contact you first is if you want reassurance that he's into it. But if you don't need that for your own peace of mind, feel free to get in touch with him.

If a guy likes you, he wants to hear from you—don't worry about messing things up by contacting him first. One guy told me: "I think it's impressive when a girl is the first to call or text. It shows confidence, and it's refreshing. It's not like guys aren't self-conscious. It's nice to know the girl is interested." A 23-year-old added: "If I like a girl, I definitely want to hear from her. If she texts me, that's great. Calling would be fine too, but I feel like most of the time girls won't do that."

Sometimes we forget that a guy's feelings don't hinge on a text message or a phone call. By the time you've been on a date or two with a guy, he's formed an opinion about whether he likes you or not. He's not going to all of a sudden stop liking you because you got in touch with him. Like, "I went on a date with this girl I liked. But then, oh my god, she sent me a text! What the hell? Where does she get off?" Feelings don't work like that. If a guy likes you, he likes you; and if he doesn't, he doesn't. These little things that are so easy to obsess over (like whether or not to text or call) aren't actually going to derail a potential relationship.

If it's been more than a week since your date, and you haven't heard from a guy, chances are you aren't going to. This is another time when you might want to text or call him. Intimidating, yes, but getting in touch with a guy can only influence the outcome for the better (or not at all). If he doesn't like you, the battleship is already sunk, so it doesn't matter. If he wasn't sure enough about his feelings to get back in touch, your contacting him creates the potential for a second date, and a second chance. And if he didn't call because he wussed out and thought you weren't interested, then it's good you reached out. If you thought a date went well and there was a connection, wouldn't you rather make one last effort instead of sitting around wondering "what if?" And if he doesn't respond after you put yourself out there, then you can cut your losses and move on. He deserves a second chance to show interest, but not a third, fourth, or fifth.

Can I Text/Call Him Between Dates, or Is That Needy and Annoying?

If you're like many girls, there have been times you've wanted to get in touch with a guy but stop yourself because you don't want to annoy him. While an understandable fear, it's one that's completely unjustified. Assuming he's into you, he's going to be excited to see your name come across his phone, just like you get excited when his name comes across yours.

On the follow-up survey, I asked guys if they wanted to be contacted in between dates by a girl they've been out with a few times. I gave them a few different answers and asked them to check all that apply. Only 2% said they preferred to be the one making contact. A full 67% said it's nice to hear from a girl you like (without any restrictions on how they wanted to be contacted). Only 5% of guys said they wanted to hear from a girl via text only (hold the calls, please). And 20% said they wanted mostly texts, and occasional calls. A guy who likes you wants to hear from you; you don't have to worry about "bothering" him or looking stalkerish. Crazy, I know, but guys actually have feelings for girls they date and are excited, yes, just to talk to them.

Whenever you're having that "should I call or not" dilemma, remember that getting in touch will never be the straw that breaks the camel's back or pushes a guy over the edge of deciding he doesn't like you. If you want to say hi, tell him something funny that happened to you, or just see how he's doing, reach out. But before you go ape shit blowing up his celly, a few addendums.

Addendums...

When you first start dating someone, the relationship is still in the information-gathering stage. Therefore, you don't want to do anything that looks crazy, because a guy doesn't know you well enough to know that you're not. While you shouldn't worry at all about being the one to make contact, stay within these (mostly common sense) parameters.

1. IT SHOULDN'T BE EXCESSIVE.

A guy who likes you wants you to get in touch with him—I cannot stress that enough. What he doesn't want is you calling him 20 times a day (just like you don't want some guy you've been on a few dates with to start doing that to you—a sure sign of psycho). On the online survey 26% of guys said *initiating* contact every day was excessive. Initiating contact multiple times a day was excessive to 42% of guys, and 32% said excessive was texting before they've responded back, or after they've responded with short answers showing they can't talk.

Excessive also has to do with content. One guy told me: "I want to hear from a girl if I like her, but at the same time I don't want to hear from her incessantly about nothing." When you first start dating someone, there's no need to text him every thought that pops into your head or every move you make that has no relation to him: "I have no food in my fridge." "Think I'm going to eat a burrito for breakfast, is that weird?" "My foot itches." "My abs are sore from this class at the gym, LOL." If you're worried about annoying a guy when initiating contact, just stick to messages that relate to him in some way.

Use your judgment, and pay attention to the signs you're getting back. According to one 24-year-old: "If I start texting back really short answers that don't ask a question, it means I'm busy or don't feel like talking." If you're getting short responses, take it as a hint it's time to end the conversation. This isn't a hard hint to take under normal circumstances, but if you've had a few cold ones and are missing your guy, that's the time you have to be careful of plowing through the obvious "stop texting me" signals. If you're an overly chatty drunk, give your phone to a friend so you won't even be tempted. The things you do when you're drunk still count, and you will regret them the next day—even if it doesn't feel like it at the time.

2. IT SHOULDN'T LOOK DESPERATE.

A guy whose dating life I followed had hooked up with a girl twice when her texts started getting out of control. She started initiating conversations several times a day, and even after he texted back short answers like, "yeah" and "ha-ha," she wouldn't get the hint and continued to text him. He didn't want to be rude, so he kept responding, but only with one-word answers and he never wrote a question back. (This girl was definitely violating addendum 1.) The real kicker came when she started sending messages that to him looked desperate: "I hope you don't mind, but when I get drunk I send sexts."

He took this move as a clear cry for attention. It would have been one thing if they had been in an established relationship. Instead, he saw this as a desperate attempt to win him over using sex after picking up the vibe that he wasn't that into her. Basically, it's a cheap shot. That, most important, doesn't work. Guys aren't actually controlled by their penises (more on this later), and trying to lure a guy who doesn't seem that interested with the promise of sex just isn't a successful strategy.

How Often Am I Gonna See This Guy?

So you're in the gray area, where it would be almost as awkward to say a guy's not your boyfriend as it would be to say he is. You've been on enough dates that you'd feel weird going out with someone else, but it hasn't been quite long enough to have the "what are we" discussion. The expectations for this stage of a relationship are entirely unclear, which makes deciding how much time and effort to put in especially annoying.

This is particularly problematic when deciding how much you're supposed to see your not-really/not-really-not boyfriend. If you already have plans to see him on Saturday, can you invite him to something Friday night, or is that too much? On the follow-up survey I asked guys how often they expected to see a girl they had been on a few dates with (and liked). At this stage of a relationship,

11% of guys expect to see a girl just once a week, 55% said once or twice, 27% said twice or three times, and 7% said three or more times a week.

If it looks like a relationship is going somewhere, 89% of guys assume you'll hang out more than once each week. So don't feel tentative about doubling (or even tripling) up on plans. The numbers have spoken, your guy wants to see you.

I would also take these numbers to mean that if you've been dating a guy for a while but don't see him that often, he's probably not looking to start a relationship with you. While collecting surveys in Battery Park in NYC, I got into a discussion about relationship labels with a girl who's guy friend was filling out a survey. She was assuming that a guy she had been dating for three months was her boyfriend even though they had never officially talked about it. At first I agreed with her, that possibly he just felt awkward about having the actual conversation. Then, I found out that she's 24, he's 30, they only see each other "almost once a week" on "most weekends," and they *never* hang out during the week (or talk much either) because "he's really busy." Knowing this, I'd be very surprised if he considered her his girlfriend.

A relationship should look like a relationship. That means it should progress. After three months, you should definitely be seeing a guy more than "usually once a week." Most guys expect to see a girl more than that after only a couple of dates.

Mind-blowing, but guys actually want to hang out with a girl they're into! You're not bothering or burdening a guy by wanting to see him. Believe me, a single guy doesn't have better things to do with his time. Most likely, a guy you've just started dating isn't trying to see you more because he doesn't want to look like he's harassing *you*.

CASE STUDY: JIM

You know those horror movies where it seems like they're over but then the bad guy isn't actually dead and pops out and starts stabbing people again? That's kind of what researching this book has been like. Just when I think I'm done collecting information, I start talking to a guy and realize there's more.

Weeks into the editing process, I met Jim, a 41-year-old from the Boston area, in a hotel lobby in New York. I was waiting for a friend, he was having an after-dinner drink, and the chair next to him was the only seat in the house. Jim wanted what all 41-year-olds in hotel bars want—to buy you a drink and talk about their divorce.

"I had doubts about my relationship the day I got married," he said. "I knew it wasn't right."

"Then why did you do it?" I asked.

"Because I wanted kids. I always knew I wanted kids. And now that I have them they're the most important things in my life. Two years ago when I left my wife, my daughter said, 'Daddy, you ruined my perfect life.' It broke my heart, but I had such a miserable relationship I just couldn't stay. I still live in the same town as my ex, and every choice I've made since the divorce has been to try to keep my kids happy. They mean everything to me. I had a really great day with my daughter a few weeks ago, and she said, 'Daddy, thanks for making my life perfect again.' That meant so much." Jim looked like he might start crying.

"Wait a minute. Sorry to change the subject, but can we go back to the marriage thing for a second? You married the wrong woman just because you wanted kids?"

"Yep."

"That seems kinda severe. I mean, I want kids too, but I'm not about to marry the wrong guy to do it."

"Yeah, but you're a girl."

"So?"

"So you can have kids whenever you want to. I can't."

Guys can't have kids! A completely obvious statement, but think about the implications this has on dating! We always hear about how dating is hard for women as they get older because they're up against the pressures of their biological clock. But when we hit our late 30s, even if there are no prospects on the horizon, if we want to, we can have kids by ourselves. Go to a sperm bank, have a lot of unprotected sex with virile men, or talk a good friend into impregnating us . . . If we want to get knocked up, we can probably do it.

Guys can't. And according to a recent study by Match.com, men are actually more likely to say they want kids than women. But to get those kids, they pretty much need us. Sure, they can try to adopt. But that's a very selective process, and a single guy probably doesn't have the best shot. Guys don't have the upper hand because of our biological clock; we have the upper hand because we have a clock in the first place! So the idea that dating is tricky for women as we get older but not men is a total crock— it's just another lie that makes guys look as though they have more power than they actually do. As you get older, dating is more difficult because there's more at stake. That's just as true for guys as it is for us.

LA: Swine

. . . .

"I'm sorry to bother you, and this is going to sound kind of strange, but do either of you know a place around here where guys might be hanging out?"

I had been driving around LA for hours and, based on a bad tip, ended up at the completely deserted Beverly Center. Not being able to face getting back into my car, I decided to scour the surrounding strip mall just in case there was some treasure trove of men that I had missed. When I saw two 20-something guys walking down the street, I pounced.

They looked confused by my request, but after I explained myself, they seemed infinitely less sketched out. "We're on our way to our office around the corner with seven guys who fit your criteria. You're welcome to come in if you want."

I took them up on their offer, passed out my surveys, and accidentally started a heated debate about what men look for in women. I spent the next hour in a chair in the middle of their makeshift office swinging my head from one side of the room to the other as two of the guys (verbally) duked it out.

On my left, a 28-year-old with a law degree. Listening to him talk was like being in every woman's worst nightmare of how shallow guys might actually be. His basic take on women: "I go out to the club looking for the hottest girl I can find. You know, model types. Skinny with big boobs. Some guys like the really skinny girls, like where you can see their bones. Personally I'm not into that." Well, thank God! (For a second there I was worried I was talking to a guy with no standards!) He went on, "I would never want to be in a relationship, because what if there's another girl out there I could get with who's even hotter?"

In the middle of the room was one of the guys who brought me into the office. During the "I want to score hot girls" rant, he would make eye contact with me, roll his eyes, and shake his head. "He does not speak for all of us. That is not how I feel at all . . ."

To my right was a guy who had just started dating a girl he was clearly very into. I think he was more offended by his co-worker's comments than I was. He was full-on screaming at him: "You are so full of shit! There is no way you actually think like that. Who are you trying to impress here? That is so beyond ridiculous." And then, he launched into a rant of his own—one that deserves to be the climax of the next blockbuster romcom.

"I'm a glutton. In every sense of the word. I stuff my face with unhealthy food, I'm lazy, I drink a lot, I'm driven to have sex all the time. But when I care about a girl, she makes me a better form of myself. I want to control my impulses, and not give in to every gluttonous desire. This girl I'm dating now, I respect her so much. She keeps kosher and that's something I've never had the urge or willpower to do, because I just love food too much. But being with her, man . . ." He paused and shook his head. "She makes me want to not eat pork."

Does He Like Me? Is This
Going Anywhere? And Can
I Ask Him What's Up?

KNOWING IF
HE'S INTERESTED

How Will I Know
If He Really Likes Me?

Remember that guy friend of yours from high school? The kind of
dweeby one in the Airwalks you had absolutely no interest in, but
who clearly had the biggest crush on you? How did you know that
he liked you? He was certainly too shy to ever explicitly tell you
to your face. But you knew anyway because it was completely
obvious.

We can spend so much time and energy debating whether the
guys we like are into us or not, but we tend to forget that when a
guy likes you it's sort of clear—somewhere deep down there, you
just . . . know.

Two hundred and ninety-nine guys who filled out the survey wrote in an explanation of how they treat a girl differently if they're into her and want to pursue a relationship. And out of that 299, only three indicated that they don't show interest. The other 296 guys wrote in answers that can be summarized by the words "more" and "better." While the guys who play hard to get are certainly out there, it seems that if they're interested in starting something real, they drop the charade (or at least downsize it).

According to what guys wrote on their surveys, when a guy likes you he will act "more attentive," "more charming," "more caring," will be a "better listener," "more interested in your life or values," "more respectful," "more patient," and just "overall nicer." Guys are going to try harder and show you their intentions through planned-out dates, deeper conversations, and more thoughtful actions because, as one 28-year-old said: "When you like a girl, you do it right." How refreshingly straightforward: A guy who likes you is going to act more interested.

The only way that a guy might act *less* interested is that he may hold off having sex with you. About 15% of guys mentioned that when they want a relationship with a girl they take it slower physically. (It's that strange phenomenon that it's "fine" to sleep with the ones we don't like, but we feel we should delay it with the ones we do.)

How soon do guys know if they like a girl? Two-thirds (68%) who took the original survey said they treat a girl differently *from the beginning* if they want a relationship with her. Many guys decide right away if they want to date you or just hook up with you. How a guy treats you (even at the very beginning) is often a good indication of his intentions.

So does this guy like you? I don't know, you tell me. No, seriously. Does it feel like he likes you? Does he contact you on a regular basis, make himself available, and try to set up dates? Does he pay attention to you and treat you well when you're together? Is he constantly showing signs that he's interested? Do you feel liked?

When a guy is interested in you, more often than not he's going to be acting in a way that makes that clear. Just like you could tell who had a crush on who in high school, people's feelings are just as transparent when they're older. So if you can look at your relationship objectively (which is the true challenge here), a guy's feelings will be clear.

How Will I Know If He's No Longer Feeling It?

If the signs a guy likes you can be summarized by the word *more*, then the signs he doesn't like you can be summarized by the word *less*. On the following page are the signals guys say indicate they've lost interest in a girl they've been seeing:

"If you've lost interest in a girl you've been seeing, what are the signs?"

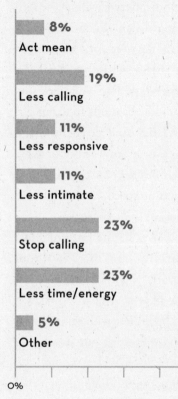

8%
Act mean

19%
Less calling

11%
Less responsive

11%
Less intimate

23%
Stop calling

23%
Less time/energy

5%
Other

0%   100%

When a guy loses interest after a few dates, almost a quarter are just going to stop calling you. That sign, while rude, is at least hard to miss. A good majority of the guys who are left over are just going to call you less, make less of an effort to see you, stop trying to make plans with you, and take a longer time to respond to your texts or calls. If a guy used to call a lot and now barely checks in, that's a sure sign the relationship is going south. As one guy wrote, "If I like you, I will be contacting you somehow with regularity."

Other guys are going to show their disinterest by how they interact with you. They're going to be more distant, initiate less physical contact, or just generally act cold. In the words of a 38-year-old in LA: "Signs I've lost interest in a girl? Same for most guys—around less, less sex, less attention, less everything." A 28-year-old lawyer in Atlanta said that when he no longer wants to date a girl he starts "acting out, pushing boundaries, and generally doing things to make her begin to want out, or at least sense there are problems and the end may be near." If instead of acting happy to see you, a guy has a "short fuse," "acts annoyed," or is "just less friendly," the outlook of your relationship is likely bleak.

If you're struggling through a "he loves me/he loves me not" dating situation, the best advice I can give you is to go with your gut. The majority of the time, deep down, you know. Because just like a guy makes it obvious when he likes you, he also makes it obvious when he doesn't. If you can be honest with yourself, his feelings are probably clear. And if you're freaking out about a relationship, there's likely a reason.

This is not to say that your freaking out is a definite sign that things are headed downhill. Everyone gets spooked every now and then. If you had a normal conversation with him two hours ago and don't have any solid support to back up your worries, refocus your energy on global warming, homelessness, or something that's actually a problem. But if you're constantly freaking out, and then constantly having to make excuses for why he might be acting a certain way, that's the sign of a problem. And in that case, you need to be more honest with yourself. If he was treating you the way he was supposed to, you wouldn't be worried, and you wouldn't have to keep justifying his actions.

As complicated as people are, I think the majority of us act in ways that stay true to our feelings (even if we're not completely aware of them). In that way, people are simple. If he's acting like he doesn't like you, most likely he doesn't. If his actions are telling you something, don't rationalize them; recognize them. And if your gut is telling you something, don't try to talk yourself out of it—listen.

How Do I Know If He's Just Playing Hard to Get?

Less calling, less planning to see you, less intimacy, and less nice are all bad signs in a dating relationship. But what if you've *just* started seeing a guy and don't know what his "less" is?

Body language experts talk about the importance of base lining. That is, you can't read into people's actions based on one situation, you have to look at their actions within the context of their history. A guy might try to see you "less" than the last guy you dated. But that doesn't mean anything. You can only tell if a guy is acting "less interested" by comparing his current actions to how he acted before, something that's impossible to do with a guy you don't know that well. And to complicate matters further, there are plenty of guys out there who subscribe to "the more you ignore her, the more she'll like you" philosophy. This means that in order to gauge the interest of a guy you've just started dating, you may have to recognize the difference between a guy who's playing hard to get and one who's just uninterested.

According to a 29-year-old in Boston: "Playing hard to get isn't not returning calls or texts. Hard to get means taking a while to respond and not jumping the second a girl calls, but you do respond eventually." His definition was right in line with how other guys explained it as well. Basically, a guy playing it cool acts like he sort of wants to see you. A guy who's uninterested probably won't act like he wants to see you at all.

Many guys also said that if they're acting intentionally aloof, they'll sack up after a while and stop being so annoying. Says one 27-year-old: "You try to act like you don't care and treat a girl with indifference so that she likes you. It takes a couple of weeks; then you realize that the girl is going to like you anyway, so you act more like how you feel." A guy who likes you will act more interested as time goes on. One who doesn't like you won't.

If a guy wants to date you, he will be actively trying to see you, even if he's trying to play hard to get. He may not take you up on every invitation, get in touch with you every day, or respond to you right away. But the general trend of his actions will be that he's keeping in touch and trying to make plans. Determining the difference between hard to get and uninterested ultimately boils down to looking at the bigger picture. Either he's making an effort (even a half-assed one) or he's not.

Why Is He Texting Me but Not Actually Trying to See Me?

The worst part of any dating situation is being in limbo—not knowing if he's interested or not, and overanalyzing each word in your last communication. Here's your current dilemma: He's not making any effort to meet up with you, but he always responds to your texts, and occasionally says cute things back. He's giving you the text and bail: "I'm going to text you back, but bail on any effort to actually move things forward." This is the one move capable of producing the thought: "If he's not into it, I wish he would just flat out ignore me." But he doesn't. He half ignores you. So it's "He loves me, he loves me not, he loves me, he loves me not, he loves me . . . piece of shit—stop keeping in touch with me if we're not going to actually meet up!"

The million-dollar question: Why is he doing it? And unfortunately, there's no one definitive answer I can give you. But I can give you your odds, so like any capable gambler, you'll have an idea of where to place your bet.

On the original survey I asked guys: "You've been on a few dates with a girl/hooked up with her a few times. You always return her texts but don't make any plans to actually see her. Why?" First of all, it's important to know that 21% of guys said they would never be in this situation—that they wouldn't be texting a girl they weren't going to make an effort to see. But for the guys who would, or have, this is why:

"Why are you texting a girl but making no plans to meet up?"

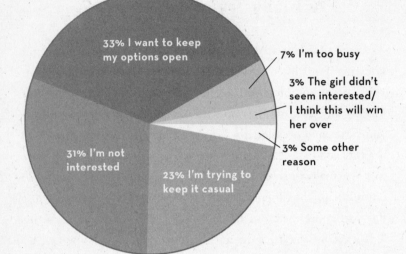

33% I want to keep my options open

7% I'm too busy

3% The girl didn't seem interested/ I think this will win her over

3% Some other reason

31% I'm not interested

23% I'm trying to keep it casual

As many excuses as we can make describing scenarios for why a guy might be interested but acting this way (maybe I'm not showing him I want to see him enough, I need to put myself out there more, he's just playing hard to get), they are true only 3% of the time.

A guy genuinely is too busy to hang out 7% of the time. And while that's no reflection of his feelings about you, his schedule is still negatively affecting your life. That's something you need to consider when thinking about moving forward. If you meet someone during an unusually hectic point in his life, or during a busy month at work, that's one thing. But dating/hooking up with a guy who is chronically busy will at best turn into a boyfriend who's chronically busy. If being in a relationship with a guy who has only a little bit of time for you is a situation you're okay with, fine. But if that doesn't sound like your ideal relationship, then I'd throw this fish back and try to catch another one.

About a third (31%) of the time, a guy isn't making an effort to meet up with you because he's just not interested. Which begs the question, "Then why are you texting me back, ass face?" And this is where the real explanations come in. Roughly a quarter of the guys who weren't interested mentioned they texted back because they didn't want to be rude. They don't want to lead you on by trying to see you, but they don't want to be impolite and ignore you. This seems to come into play the most when the guy in question is in your circle of friends or you guys are friends of friends. The rest of the "uninterested" guys were likely motivated by one of the other main responses.

Almost a quarter (23%) of guys will keep in touch with you but not try to see you because they're trying to hold the relationship where it is and keep it casual. They enjoy hanging out or hooking up, but they don't see it headed for anything serious. As summarized by one guy: "There are girls I'll date, but wouldn't want to be exclusive with."

A full third of guys (33%) stay in touch because they want to keep their options open. One guy wrote: "I'm probably unsure how far I want the relationship to go. I might be exploring other options. Doesn't mean I'm not into her, but I'm just not sure how much." Other guys (about a quarter of this group, and 8% of guys overall) were less noble, and pretty clearly stated they wanted the option of hooking up with you if they felt like it, and a text here and there would keep that door open.

The reality is, and many guys wrote this exactly, "texting is too easy." It takes such minimal effort to text someone back that many will do it to keep you around as an option "just in case," even if, as many guys admitted, there are "other girls in the picture" they like more. Basically, some guys just don't want to burn their bridges—which is selfish, yes, but something we've probably done at some point as well.

Here's the big picture: This guy you're continuing to text, there's a 31% chance he doesn't like you at all. There's a 56% chance (23% + 33%) he's either trying to keep you as something casual, or isn't interested enough to pursue anything unless things with other girls fall through. And these numbers combined is what I'd call an 87% chance it's time to move on. The only other likely reason he's not trying to see you is that he's too busy, which, as just discussed, has its own set of complications.

Now, this is where personal responsibility comes into play. How do you feel about him? How do you *really* feel about him? If he's really just a casual option for you, fine. But if he's more (and be honest with yourself about this), get out! As they say, "Never let a guy become your priority while allowing yourself to become his option."

Walking away from a guy you like is a hard thing to do. But if he's not making an effort, you have to do it. When you don't, you just whittle away at your self-esteem. I don't care how confident you are, when you like a guy and he's treating you badly, it makes you feel like crap. And it could be a really kind, sweet guy you like, but if his actions are making you feel like crap, he's making you feel like crap.

Sure, you can hang on, keep sending him texts, and keep re-arranging your schedule in hopes of seeing him. But you're just going to get let down again and again until he finally stops responding. Then, you'll have had months of disappointment ending with *him* getting to decide that *he's* had enough. Or, you'll have months of disappointment capped off with him coming over one night wanting to hook up with you, only to be followed by more disappointment.

Your other option is to take the power back, and make the choice to walk away. Though it takes a huge amount of willpower to give up on a guy you like, you will walk away feeling empowered because you put your foot down and said, "That's not how guys treat me." And money-back guarantee here, you will feel better immediately. At first, because you had the willpower to stand up for yourself. Later because there's not some schmuck who's letting you down every weekend. And even later after that when you find a guy who's making you a priority, instead of just wasting your time.

We've Been Dating for a While, So Why Isn't He Asking Me to Be His Girlfriend?

In New York I met a guy who spent many years in France and said the French are completely perplexed by the dating/hookup scene in the States.

"The French think the way we deal with relationships is absurd. We make such a huge deal out of calling someone our boyfriend or girlfriend, and then there are all these giant expectations that come along with the label. It's because we've made it into this huge deal that we have to be *sooo* sure we want to be exclusive with someone. But really, the label should just mean 'someone you're fucking while you're not fucking anyone else.' That's what a relationship is, that's not a giant commitment, and that's not too much to ask of someone."

He's right. We're so hysterical about "not rushing the relationship talk" because we've made the idea of having one out to be such a big step. Yes, having a label is a commitment, but it's not like you're vowing to fall in love or stay committed forever—you're just vowing to stay monogamous for a period of time. And if you change your mind in a month or two and decide it was a bad call, it's a vow that can be easily undone. Stores with strict return policies can make buying a dress a bigger commitment than officially having a boyfriend. But because we've built relationships up to be such a *huge* deal, having "the talk" to make one official is something that can get delayed until months into dating someone.

Many of my own relationships officially began with a guy sheepishly uttering: "Hey, this is an awkward thing to bring up . . ." With that intro, I'd worry he was going to reveal some strange fetish or something, but then he'd continue: "Can I call you my girlfriend?" Oh, pshhhhh, that's all he wanted?

It's crazy that the girlfriend/boyfriend conversation can make people so uncomfortable. Is it really that awkward to tell a girl you've been dating (and are probably sleeping with) that you like her and want to be exclusive? For some, I guess so, because according to my survey, it's the awkwardness factor that keeps 17% of guys from having "the talk" with the girl they've been dating.

Stereotypically, we assume guys don't want relationships, and that we might "scare a guy off" by pushing for one. Ironically, some guys have this same fear about us. Being unsure that the girl they're dating wants a commitment is keeping 18% of guys from initiating the relationship talk.

Six percent of the guys I surveyed just think that labels are unimportant, so there's no need for a discussion about it. Another 5% complained about some other type of baggage: being "emotionally damaged," "fearing commitment," "not wanting to commit unless you absolutely have to," or similar issues that generally indicated they're just not boyfriend material. And 54% of guys said the most likely reason they hadn't had "the talk" with a girl they've been seeing is that they weren't sure they wanted to have a relationship with her.

What all these percentages boil down to is that when a guy you've been dating for a while isn't calling you his girlfriend, there's about a 60% chance it's because he's not ready to commit to you. And there's about a 40% chance he's not saying anything because he's too much of a wuss to have the conversation (or a slight chance he thinks labels are stupid and unnecessary and when someone is your girlfriend, it's obvious).

Of the 60% who aren't sure they want a commitment, some just need more time. There's a very good chance a guy not calling you his girlfriend is nothing to be concerned about at all (especially because we can be so hysterical about giving something a label). As long as your guy is showing all the signs that he's into it, there's no need to worry. And if he's giving you mixed signals, you can always ask him point-blank: "Where do you see this headed?"

Can I Ask Where It's Going, or Will That Be the Kiss of Death for Our Relationship?

Getting guys to fill out a survey is one thing, but getting them to talk with you about their sex and dating lives is quite another. You would think that a girl (by herself) asking a guy to talk about sex, love, and relationships wouldn't face much opposition. Not the case. Almost every time I approached a guy sitting alone, he would look awkward, then scared, then quickly shuffle around his iPhone and say he was "too busy."

Approaching guys in a group was exactly the opposite. Safety in numbers, I guess, because instead of awkwardly saying they were busy, guys in groups would scream their consent: "Hell yeah, you can talk to us about sex! Pull up a chair, baby." Of course the bigger the group, the more bullshit you have to wade through to get real answers. Like that stat about the chances of an accident increasing exponentially with every teen added to a car, the obligatory spewing of crap goes up exponentially with every guy added to a table. They get past the sex jokes after a while, but boy, do you have to work for it. I learned it's best to find two guys sitting together. Inevitably there is one who does most of the talking, and the other is there as a bodyguard or something.

After approaching a duo in DC, a 28-year-old serial dater named Tim agreed to talk to me as he finished up his lunch. "Good timing. I just ended it with a girl last night. Sit down, have some fries." I took a seat at his table.

"So what went wrong?" I asked, descending upon his lukewarm fries.

"See, I enjoy going out and doing fun stuff with ladies, and it gets me in trouble. You know, like taking them to baseball games and stuff. Real dates. I enjoy their company. My friends' wives say it leads girls on. But can't I just spend a month or two getting to know someone? It's not fair that guys get looked at as assholes for going on 10 dates and then not wanting anything."

Fair enough. "So what does this have to do with the chick you broke up with last night?"

"Well, I was seeing this girl for a little over a month. She had been so good about not asking, 'Where is this going? How do you feel about me?' Then she brought all that up last night."

"Okay, wait a minute. 'So good about not asking'? If you really liked the girl and wanted a relationship with her, would you worry about that conversation?"

"No, not at all."

"So you only don't want a girl to ask, 'Where is this going?' if it means giving her an answer she's not going to like?"

He thought about this one for a second. "Well . . . yeah."

We're so afraid of asking guys where something is headed because we think they universally dread that question, and stop liking us the instant we ask it. But that's not true at all. Guys only dread that conversation if they don't see the relationship going anywhere and are simply enjoying your company as a way to pass the time. Asking the question may end things, but that's only because it sheds light on feelings that were already there to begin with.

Don't forget, guys want relationships (yes, I know that's the opposite of almost everything we're told). Remember that 99% of guys I surveyed said they'd want a relationship with "the right girl," and 73% said their primary interest in women is finding someone to have a relationship with. That being said, while waiting for that elusive relationship, people get lonely. And to deal with that loneliness, many will spend time hanging out with someone who they don't see a future with but are enjoying at the time. This isn't just a guy thing; girls do it too. It's human nature to seek out companionship. And that's totally fine . . . as long as both people are on the same page.

If you're unsure about where a relationship is headed and want some answers, feel free to get them. Don't ask a guy where things are going after the first date, because at that point, you don't know him well enough to know what you want either. If it's been a while, you see the guy often, talk to him regularly, and things seem to be progressing, it's totally fine to ask him what he's thinking. And you don't have to ask in a way that implies, "Commit to me now or die." You can say something that's low pressure for both of you. Something like, "Do you see this progressing into a relationship, or do you want to keep it casual?"

If you've been seeing a guy for a while and things *don't* seem to be progressing (i.e., it's been a month of weekend hookups), feel free to ask what's going on there, too. And assuming you want it to go somewhere, you really should. If he wants something casual and you want a relationship, then your Saturday nights are probably best spent elsewhere.

It is well within your right to know what sort of relationship you're involved in, and to make sure that it coincides with the type of relationship you're looking for. You shouldn't be dedicating the time and energy to treat a guy like your boyfriend if at the end of the day he doesn't want to be. And if he doesn't know what he wants, you should know that too, and from there decide if you feel like waiting around for him to figure it out. Asking, "Where is this going?" may mean getting an answer you don't want to hear. But it's always better to know than to unknowingly waste your time.

Is There Some Black Hole That Seemingly Interested Guys Get Sucked into After a Few Dates?

Every girl knows this scenario: No doubt about it, he was into you. Totally into you. He called, texted, and seemed completely smitten . . . or smitten enough, anyway. Then all of a sudden he disappeared, dropped off the face of the earth. You'd think he was dead somewhere, but the dick has been friending people on Facebook. So you replay every second of your last date over and over again in your head. He had his hand on your leg at the beginning of the night. And then halfway through he kissed you on the forehead. At what exact second did he stop liking you? What did you do wrong? What did you say? Did that zit you covered up suddenly become visible and gross him out?

If that situation doesn't ring a bell, then perhaps this one does: You've been on three dates with a guy. They went well. He's reliable, fun, and you feel like this one has potential. So on the fourth date you sleep with him. Then poof. He goes dark. Could it get any more cliché?

What the hell happens to these guys? Where do they go? Oh, to get your hands on that black box flight recorder to figure out how and why it all went down. But deafening silence is the new dumped, because something that doesn't have a label doesn't deserve a breakup. As so eloquently put by an attractive off-duty cop, "The not-call-back thing is so rude, but it's become acceptable. It eventually boils down to emotional cowardice. I don't want to have to break up with someone I've only been on a few dates with. I don't want to have to say, 'You're a great person, but I just don't see this heading for a relationship.'"

It's annoying, but at least clear what it means when a guy stops calling. And to be fair, many of us have done it too. Honestly, maybe it is better than suffering through a conversation of "I don't think this is going to work out." But the real question is: Why? Why did things seem to be going so well, or why did they end right after sex?

Here is why they seemed to be going well: If a first date goes horribly and you clearly hate each other, it ends right there and then. "If it makes it past a first date," says one 24-year-old, "you probably like the girl. If you see her regularly, you should know more after a few weeks." So on the next few dates a guy knows he likes you. The question he's now asking is: How much? And even if the answer is ultimately "not enough," during this trial dating period, a guy is probably going to flirt and act interested—because acting any other way would be both rude and awkward. But this act can be a bit misleading, since the truth is, he's not 100% sold. So while on the surface it may look like everything is going great, in reality he is still actively evaluating if it's a good match.

Many guys said it takes about three to four dates to get to know a girl and decide if they want things to progress. Even the DC 10-date-serial-dater admitted he was pretty sure of his feelings by date four. So if you stop hearing from a guy after a few dates that seemed to go well, it's because he's realized that while he enjoys your company, ultimately it's not headed anywhere—either that, or his ex is back in the picture (no stats on this one, just an abundance of anecdotal evidence).

Unfortunately, around the third or fourth date may also be when you decide to sleep with him. If you don't sleep with a guy until you have solidified your feelings about him, it would make sense that in this time frame he has also started to solidify his feelings about you. And what sex can do is either force a relationship decision, or serve as the icing on the proverbial "I'm not into it" cake.

Many guys told me that if they're on the fence about a girl, sleeping with her can bring them to the "this isn't going to work" realization a little quicker. Why? Because sex is an intimate act. And when you do it with someone you don't really like, it's just kinda gross. So what may have been a hazy "no" before, becomes a very clear "I'm not into this, and it never needs to happen again." Not that it takes sex to reach that conclusion, though. Many guys said they would have gotten there eventually, but that sex sped things up.

The other thing sex can do is make a guy feel forced to evaluate a relationship because, as one said, "You need to decide sooner how serious it is." Likely because of the assumption that girls have sex for emotional reasons (not physical ones), some guys take the fact that you slept with them as a demonstration of your commitment. Many then feel pressured to let you know if that commitment is something they want to reciprocate.

There's this idea that guys leave after sex because they've "gotten what they wanted." But I'd say that's rarely the case. Yes, there is that 5% to 10% of guys who are emotionally repressed (and 100% confused about how to make themselves happy). For those guys, sure, that argument carries some weight. But for the vast majority of guys, it doesn't. Think about it: If sex was really all they wanted, it would make them stay. You don't work your ass off at a job, finally get a promotion, and then go, "Okay, got what I wanted, I quit." For the most part, guys disappearing after sex isn't about having gotten what they wanted, as much as realizing that they've gotten something they don't.

Chicago: All Signs Point to Nowhere

After spending all summer traveling, I coordinated my visit to Chicago to overlap with my boyfriend's trip to see his sister and parents.

It turned out to be the weekend from hell.

Two years into our relationship, and we had never had a major fight. Now, here in Chicago the first afternoon, shit hits the fan. Two years' worth of shit, and I'm seeing red—standing in an alley somewhere so pissed I don't even care that I'm "that girl" sobbing on the street. I can't even smile about the irony that I'm there to do research for a book about the fact that guys "aren't really that bad." The worst part is: I'm supposed to be at dinner with his parents in a few hours.

Fights are never about what they're about. And the insensitive act that set this one off was really just a microcosm for what had become an entire relationship that revolved around his insensitivity.

The real issue, and I can only see this now after months of distance from the situation, is that we were having a relationship that he wasn't ready for. Maybe because I was his first serious girlfriend? Or because his job was unstable? Or maybe because deep down, he knew I just wasn't "the one." I may never know why. He may never know why. But the result was a relationship he was faking his way through. If it had been a college class, he skipped all the lectures, copied the notes from a friend, and studied them just long enough to pass the final exam.

He gave me sign after sign that he wasn't feeling the relationship, but I ignored them and pressed on. When I stopped making an effort to go out with his friends, we didn't spend a night out together for four months. Together, we only did things he wanted to do—though I was free to do anything I wanted on my own. It wasn't our life, it was his life, and I fit into it . . . sort of.

He'd say that he knew he didn't appreciate me, and he confessed that many days when he came home he just wanted to be alone. When I brought up living together (since we essentially had been for the past six months), his first response was "Do we have to?" I'd complain about it being too cold in his apartment: "Would you turn down the AC, sweetie? It's freezing in here." He'd say: "I know a place that's not freezing. It starts with *east* and rhymes with *pillage*." (My apartment was in the East Village.)

Everything with him came out as a joke. And I failed to see that like most jokes, the reason they're funny is because they illuminate some underlying truth. In this case, the truth was that I occupied more space in his life than he cared to allot.

But on the other hand, he said he loved me, and that he wanted the relationship to work. Clearly, I wasn't the only one ignoring the obvious signs that would point to a different conclusion. It may not have ended until Atlanta, but had we been honest with ourselves, by Chicago we could have realized the relationship was over.

We overcomplicate things, but reading situations can be deceivingly simple. People are honest with their emotions. Not necessarily because we want to be, but because at the end of the day, we act in ways that are a true reflection of how we feel. Words are important. But actions always speak louder. Because looking at what people do is the clearest indication of what they actually want.

CASE STUDY: BEN

I texted Ben: "In an odd twist of events, I'm reaching out to you to talk about my guy problems. Let me know if you can grab a beer."

We had casually mentioned trying to hang out when I was in Chicago, but even with no solid plans I knew that when I texted him in crisis, he'd be there. Even though when it comes down to it, he owes me nothing. If anything, I'm indebted to him for taking the time to keep me abreast of all of his romantic encounters. But that's Ben, always there, whether you deserve it or not.

Sure enough, he texted me back immediately, directed me to a party on his brother's roof deck, and greeted me with some majorly disgusting, prepackaged rum drink. Hey, beggars can't be choosers.

Ben is a 25-year-old I met when he was visiting friends in New York, and after talking briefly, he agreed to let me follow his love life. At this point we've been in touch for a year and a half and I've gotten almost bimonthly updates on all of his various lady friends.

Most of the other guys I followed I'd basically have to stalk. "Hey, hope all is well. I'd really like to chat this week if you have 20 minutes." "Hey, don't know if you got my last e-mail, I'd love to catch up, hear what's going on. Anytime works for me." "Sorry to harass you, but I'd really like to touch base."

But not with Ben. Ben would actually e-mail me: "It's been two weeks—what day do you want to chat? Below are some notes I took on what's been going on. Tuesday or Wednesday works best on my end."

I have no idea what Ben's performance is like at work, but from a personal standpoint, he's an overachiever. He goes above and beyond for everyone. So much so that you take him for granted. You literally can't help it. I never went through the trouble of reaching out to him for an interview, because I knew he'd be on top of it to set things up.

When I saw him in Chicago it had been about a year since we first met. He showed me the view from the top of his brother's building, and then we went in search of a quiet place to chat. We ended up sitting on exercise equipment in the empty gym for a scene that looked like the beginning of a bad porno. I told him my boyfriend drama with enough background information that he could understand why I was so upset.

His advice: "Well, I guess you just have to put on a happy face and act like everything is okay since his parents are here and all."

"Are you crazy? That's the worst advice ever. I'm not one to cause a scene, especially in front of someone's parents. But what he did was really wrong. And that on top of our entire relationship, where he's put in only mediocre effort! No! I'm not going to do him any favors after he just did something shitty to me. I refuse to suck it up and hang out with him all weekend just so that he doesn't have to give an uncomfortable explanation to his parents. No freakin' way! See, this is why you get screwed over by girls . . . oh my god . . . that's it! This is why you get screwed over by girls!"

I have an entire composition notebook filled with detailed accounts of every date and hookup that Ben has had in the past eighteen months. The common thread: He is continually being taken advantage of by girls he really likes. He puts in all this effort, they do nothing, he continues to bend over backward, and at the end of the day they say: "Let's just be friends."

Ben's attractive, funny . . . he has a job. There's no reason why he shouldn't be doing better with the ladies. And he does fine, but just not with the ones he really likes. When he really likes a girl, he basically lies down at her feet and says, "Let me be your door-mat." But no one wants someone to walk on; they want someone to walk with. I think one guy nailed it on the head when he wrote: "Most guys are nice to women. Unfortunately they give in too much. That is weak. So girls go for jerks because at least they have a spine." When he likes a girl, Ben has no spine. So in spite of all his other positive characteristics, they lose interest.

Being considerate in relationships is a good thing. But only up to a point—and that point is when being considerate for some-one else means being inconsiderate to yourself. If someone isn't treating you well, you can't just ignore it and act like everything is fine. When someone isn't putting forth the same amount of effort, you can't carry the extra weight and keep giving more. It doesn't work two weeks into dating, and apparently it doesn't work two years into dating either.

In order for someone to be interested in you, you have to have a backbone. You have to be willing to lay down ground rules for how you expect to be treated. And if they're not being met, aban-don the relationship, or at the very least take a step back until they are. If you don't show respect for yourself, no one else is going to show respect for you either.

When I Screwed Him Last Night, Did I Also Screw Our Shot at a Relationship?

SEX AND DATING

Will He Think I'm High Maintenance If I Don't Bounce First Thing in the Morning After a Hookup?

There's a time after a hookup when the night turns into the morning. You fell asleep hugging each other, and wake up hugging opposite sides of the bed with a vague recollection that you didn't go to sleep alone. At this point, you have two options. A, act like the night never happened: "Oh, funny meeting you here." Don't make any effort to kiss or cuddle, and quickly leave so you're not the "needy girl" who hung around all day after a hookup. B, you can refuse to separate the night from the morning, initiate some cuddling, and hang out a bit. Of course, which way do you go?

I asked guys: "The morning after a hookup, do you want the girl to leave right away?" Only 20% gave a definitive yes, get out of my face. A full 30% said no, please stay, and 50% said it depends. What it depends on, they wrote, is if they like you, if they were drunk the night before (and you're basically a stranger), how well they know you (if they know you, please stay), if it feels awkward, and if they have things to do. As a general rule, though, most guys *don't* want you to leave first thing in the morning after a hookup—especially if they see the potential for a relationship. And in the situations they'd want you to leave (how did I end up here? Who are you again?), chances are you'd want to get the hell out of there too.

If you've hooked up with a guy who you might be interested in dating, you should definitely stick around to show that you want to get to know him better. Real relationships *can* come out of first-night hookups (stats on this on page 128 and 130). But before you can start a relationship, you have to detach yourself from the left side of his *Star Wars* sheets.

What's your move? First order of business, if you're feeling awkward, snap out of it. You guys hooked up the night before, no need to act sheepish now. When you do, you give off an air of "this was a mistake, I don't actually like you, and I'd rather kill myself than smell your morning breath." That's not the impression you want to give if you're interested in dating a guy. So, scary as it may be, take the initiative to roll over, start cuddling, and show him: "I like you in the morning too."

Second, strike up a conversation. About something, anything. Ask him questions about his life, his job, his room, whatever. As one guy put it, you want to leave him with the impression, "Hey I can really talk to this girl." Or as another said, that the morning after "didn't feel awkward at all."

"Breakfast is always a good thing," a 27-year-old said about post-hookup etiquette. "If you just get up and leave, it's never cool. Guy or girl, it's like you used someone. If anyone is interested in finding a relationship, you've got to go to breakfast the next morning." So if he hasn't suggested it yet, say: "Hey, if you don't have anywhere you have to be right now, want to grab some food?" You might even get bonus points for being willing to go on a "date" the morning after without makeup or spending the time to get ready.

Taking the initiative the next morning takes guts. But if you like the guy you have to go for it. And remember, what's the worst that can happen? If you made a bad impression the night before, you have a chance to turn it around. If you made no impression at all, you have a chance to make one. If he thought you were cool, hanging out with him will just solidify that. If he's made up his mind he doesn't like you, you've already lost, so who cares. (And if that's the case, he'll probably be obviously standoffish, say "no" to breakfast, and then you can tell him, "have a nice life" and take off.)

The point is, you can't lose. If he liked you at all the night before, he wants you to stick around so that he can get to know you better. You're not burdening him with your presence; you're gracing him with your company. Says one 28-year-old: "The most important and self-serving thing a girl can do after a hookup is project an air of confidence about herself, like she is in control of her choices. In some cases, it has made me reconsider my judgment of a girl if she carried herself in a way that says, 'This is who

I am, biatch—take it or leave it.' By running away first thing in the morning, you lose that option."

I've Been Hooking Up with This Guy for a While, Is There Any Chance of Becoming His Girlfriend?

So there's this guy you like. And things are great. Sort of. I mean, you guys hook up on the weekends. But it happens almost every weekend, so he has to be into you, right? The truth of the matter is, though, you want something more. Something that looks more like a relationship. But is that possible at this point?

On the follow-up survey I asked:

"What are the chances that a serial hookup will turn into a real relationship?"

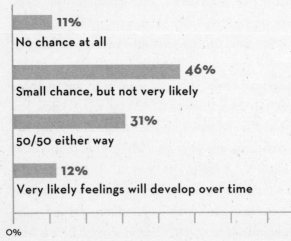

11%
No chance at all

46%
Small chance, but not very likely

31%
50/50 either way

12%
Very likely feelings will develop over time

0%   100%

The likelihood of starting a relationship with your hookup really depends on the guy as well as your specific situation. Some guys are pretty adamant about the fact that a hookup relationship cannot lead to a real relationship (11%). And more than half of guys think it's at least unlikely.

I asked a guy in Boston: "Is it possible to develop feelings for a hookup?" His response: "No. You already have a feeling developed. You're not into her, and that's why she's a booty call. If you liked her, then you'd be trying to date her."

Of course, there are a good number (43%) of guys who agreed with the thoughts of a guy in Seattle who said: "You can develop feelings for a booty call if it's a friends-with-benefits situation." That is, things might start out casually, and then over time you both realize you want something more.

But let's not delude ourselves about what a "casual relationship" or a "friends with benefits" situation actually looks like. There's "friends with benefits," and then simply "with benefits." To go back to kindergarten for a second, friends are nice to each other and respect each other's feelings. If you're hooking up with a guy who, as one wrote, "shows up hammered after ignoring you, just looking for action"—you have a "with benefits" on your hands, because that's just not very friendly. I wouldn't hold your breath for a guy like this to become your boyfriend. And most important, I know you like him, but would you really want a guy who treated you this way to be your boyfriend? (Just for reference, I lifted that quote directly from an answer to Question 14, "Signs that you're not interested in a girl.")

If, on the other hand, you have a casual relationship with a guy who's completely respectful of you, pays attention to you when you're out together, and answers your calls and texts, then you have a much higher of a chance of successfully making the transition. But a relationship isn't going to magically grow out of a hookup "Jack and the Beanstalk" style. If you want something more serious, you're going to have to demand it.

According to a 30-something in Venice Beach: "You want to be with a woman who knows what she wants and won't settle. That's sexy." If you want to turn a hookup into a relationship, your *only* move is to stop hooking up with the guy, and give him an ultimatum: "Look, I like you, and I would really like to date you and see where this goes. It's not okay with me to keep doing the occasional hookup thing. If you like me, let's try dating. But I'm done with this whole hookup situation."

The harder part then, is sticking to what you said. But you have to—for yourself, and if you want any chance of turning your hookup into your boyfriend. If you go back on your word, a guy won't respect you because he'll think he can take advantage of you. And no one will seriously date someone they don't respect. "I need a strong girl," said a 29-year-old businessman. "A girl who will call me out if I'm being sketchy and say, 'If you want to be with me, you can't act like that.'"

Might giving a guy an ultimatum end your situation completely? Absolutely. But if you want a relationship and all you're getting is a hookup, it's better that it ends. Guys want relationships (99% of them said they would want to be in one if the right girl came along). If a guy doesn't want to date you, it's because he doesn't want to date *you*, not because he doesn't want to date. And if he doesn't want to be with you, you're hooking up with a guy who's a complete waste of your time.

The bigger take-home from all of this, though, is that if you know you like a guy, the best way to get him isn't to start hooking up with him. Over half of guys say turning a serial hookup into a real relationship is at least unlikely. Old habits die hard, and it's much more difficult to steer a hookup down the relationship path than it is to start down that path to begin with. The most productive way to start a relationship is to ask a guy out. Yes, you can.

Is He Acting Like He Likes Me Just Because He Wants to Get Laid?

I went into this book believing that, romantically speaking, guys get a bad rap. So I wasn't all that surprised when the majority of my research backed up the idea that guys are people with feelings, who—like girls—care about more than just sex. What did surprise me was that the stereotype that guys will lie in order to get laid isn't actually that much of a myth. Without question, facing the reality that a significant number of guys would lie for sex was—professionally speaking—the low point of my man journey.

My first lying-related question was this: "Would you ever take a girl on a few dates, text her frequently, and fake an interest in her or her life (but not fake your willingness to have a relationship) just to get her in bed?" 56% of guys said no, and 44% of them said yes.

To me, this is not directly lying—it's a guy acting into a girl when the reality is that he's into her physically, but not emotionally. Presumably, if the girl were to ask, "Where do you see this going?" the guy would answer, "I'm not looking for anything serious," and from there she could decide if she wanted to sleep with him or not. Is it sleazy for a guy to exaggerate his interest in a girl so that she'll sleep with him? For sure. Is it abominable? Probably not.

What I really wanted to know was: How many guys would lie about their relationship intentions for sex? Do we actually have to worry about guys saying point-blank, "I like you a lot," just to get themselves laid? And this is where my heart broke. About a third of guys (35%) said they would lie about the degree of commitment they were willing to offer a girl in order to sleep with her.

The good news—and ONLY good news on this front—is that the more I asked about it, the less sketchy it got. When I put this question on the survey, this was my vision: a class-A scumbag—the type who calls everyone "babe"—telling a girl after a few dates that he wants to be exclusive just to get in her pants. But when I asked guys how they interpreted "lying about relationship intentions," it turned out that their definition of lying was much broader than mine.

According to a guy in DC: "Guys consider their actions to be lies. It's not that they would directly tell a girl they were really into her; they would just act like it when in reality they weren't totally sure." Many guys also considered avoiding the truth to be lying. If they didn't explicitly tell a girl they didn't want a relationship, they felt they had lied about their relationship intentions. I also spoke with guys who didn't believe a girl would ever want to have sex outside of a relationship. These guys literally thought that when a girl they weren't exclusively dating slept with them—in any situation—it was because they had somehow made her think a relationship was possible. They couldn't wrap their heads around the idea that maybe sex was all she wanted too.

The most rational explanation I heard about guys lying for sex was from a guy I spoke with at a bar in Atlanta: "It's not like you do it to be vindictive. You may really believe you like her at the time. There have been so many nights when I've driven drunk and believed I was okay. Then I wake up the next morning and think, 'What the hell was I doing?' It's the same with girls. Maybe you thought you liked them at the time because you were drunk."

It seems to me that when relationship intentions are lied about, for the most part it's not as direct as a guy saying, "I want to date you," and then taking it back. More likely, it's happening in alcohol-fueled situations, where a guy has just met you and is keeping his intentions deliberately vague—because the truth of the matter is, he's just trying to get some. I would also assume that of the 35% of guys who said they would lie, few make a habit of it, and many who checked "yes" did so because it's something they had done at some point (in fact, one guy even wrote that on his survey). Then, of course, there is the glass-half-full side, that almost two-thirds of guys wouldn't lie about their relationship intentions in order to score. Do all these justifications make it okay? Certainly not. But I do think they help keep this statistic in perspective.

If a guy you met at a bar is telling you between hiccups that he wants to marry you so you should come home with him—be suspicious. But don't drive yourself crazy being overly paranoid that a guy who's taken you on a few dates, seems like a sweetheart, and is showing genuine interest, is only trying to get in your pants.

What these percentages do make clear, though, is that many guys are willing to act irresponsibly when it comes to sex. One of the questions on the original survey asked guys if they felt a sense of responsibility for the emotional well-being of the girls they are romantically involved with. A full 88% of them felt *at least* somewhat responsible, and 57% said they felt very much responsible. The next question asked if they felt a sense of responsibility for the emotional well-being of the girls they've *just had sex with*. In that scenario, 62% felt at least somewhat responsible, and only 21% felt very much responsible. The reality is, when it comes to just sex, many guys don't feel like it's their job to look out for your feelings.

If there is one time to be completely skeptical of a guy, it's when you've just met him, and there's drinking involved. Those are the situations where some guys feel license to act selfishly, sleazily, and irresponsibly. So if you find yourself in that scenario, proceed with caution.

Will Having Sex with a Guy Right Away Automatically Make Me "Non-Girlfriend Material"?

While struggling to understand why guys who ultimately want girlfriends will spend their time and energy while out at bars just trying to get laid, a guy told me this:

"Every guy wants a relationship . . . That's the long-term goal. The short-term goal is to have a good weekend and have a good story to tell. Because, what's your alternative? Stay home and fill out your Match.com profile?"

Okay, I get it. It's not like a guy can stay home, meditate about having a girlfriend, and poof, one will appear. But while he's out at bars, why make a distinction between his long-term and short-term goals? Can't he pursue them both at the same time? Go out, hit on girls, piss himself, and do whatever he needs for good weekend stories—but then also consider any girl was lucky enough to sleep with as potential long-term options? You know, multitask?

Apparently it doesn't work like that (for some guys, anyway). At a tailgate for the Houston Texans, I caught a group of guys all chugging their last beer before they headed into the stadium. "One quick question," I shouted at them. "Will sleeping with a girl right away mess up the chance of a relationship?"

"No," one shouted back without missing a beat, "it blossoms the chance of a fuck buddy."

For many guys it's clear that being their "short-term goal" can exclude you from long-term possibilities. Yes, sleeping with a guy right away *can* mess up the chances of having a relationship with him. On the follow-up survey I asked:

"You meet a girl and sleep with her that night. What are the chances that it will turn into a serious relationship?"

9%
Impossible

28%
Unlikely

21%
Possible, but I'd be hesitant

35%
When I sleep with her is irrelevant

7%
None of these answers describe my feelings

0%   100%

A little over half (58%) of all guys would be at least hesitant to get involved with a girl they slept with right away. Over a third (37%) would consider relationship possibilities at least unlikely, if not impossible. And on the brighter and less judgmental end, about another third (35%) of guys aren't going to judge you based on when you have sex with them.

What makes a one-night stand more likely to turn into a relationship? In the words of many, "How well you've gotten to know each other." All casual sex is not created equal. That became apparent the more guys I spoke with. The biggest variable is the connection you make. Most guys see a distinct difference between meeting a girl and spending hours in deep conversation with her, and meeting a girl, flirting some, dancing for a while, and then taking her home. A guy from Denver said having sex right away will only mess up the chance of having a relationship "if we don't know each other. If we hung out all night, it's fine."

Sometimes, things just click. You hit it off right away, talk non-stop, and both become completely infatuated with each other. If you've managed to get to know each other really well that first night, then having sex *probably* won't change the outcome of your relationship. Even if a guy is a little hesitant about the fact you slept with him right away, many said, "If you *really* like a girl, having sex with her early on is not going to mess it up."

An important distinction to make, however, is the difference between hanging out with a guy all night, and actually getting to know him. If we're talking about a bond that was forged over shots, sloppy conversation, and some ridiculous dance moves, that's one that's likely to be washed away once the alcohol leaves your system. You may have had lots of fun together, but you probably didn't actually get to know each other that well.

As long as we're on the topic of getting it on with guys you've just met, it's worth mentioning that many guys draw a line between *sex* sex and other sexual activities. On the follow-up survey I asked:

"If you meet a girl and hook up with her that night (but don't have sex), what are the chances it will turn into a serious relationship?"

0.5%
Impossible

11%
Unlikely

23%
Possible, though I might be a little hesitant

55%
It makes no difference

11%
Other

0%   100%

Just one guy said that hooking up with a girl the night he met her would prevent a relationship, and only about a third said it would give them pause. The moral of the story here: If you're going to go home with a guy you just met, keep it above the waist.

Do Guys Refuse to Date Girls They Slept With Right Away Because They Don't Want to Date Sluts?

As I said at the beginning of the book, many guys have a screwed-up relationship with sex—way more screwed up than they realize. Part of this no doubt stems from the fact they're constantly being told how horny they are and that no guy should turn down the opportunity to bang. Add in the belief that girls only have sex for emotional reasons (because we like a guy sooo much, not because we're just plain horny), and you have the outline for our incredibly messed-up sexual landscape, and why guys can be so sexually judgmental. When talking to guys about *why* sleeping with a girl the first night can mess up relationship possibilities, these general themes emerged:

I don't want to date a girl who doesn't respect herself. If a guy believes that girls only want sex for emotional reasons, when a girl has sex before there's an emotional connection, he feels she's acting against her true desires, and therefore disrespecting herself. Guys who think this way just won't accept the idea that girls could be into sex for only physical reasons. They think if a girl has sex right away, it's because a guy somehow tricked her into it, she was desperate for attention, or she was so willing to give a guy "what he wanted" that she disregarded her own needs. This is where the whole "slut" thing comes into play. "Sluttiness" isn't really about having sex; it's about not sticking to your own standards.

I met a guy in DC who said he'd never date a girl he'd slept with right away. Unless, he concluded, she was sober when it happened. If they met at a coffee shop, she was dead sober, and she decided to have sex with him, he would respect her. The fact that she made a conscious choice and had sex because she really wanted to would take any disrespect out of the situation.

A girl who was drunk, on the other hand, he would just assume had bad judgment, poor willpower, let herself get taken advantage of, and was generally not in control of herself or her actions. Even though both of the girls ended up having sex with someone they barely knew, he would only think that the drunk girl acted "slutty."

We rarely think to separate the drunk aspect out of a one-night stand. But since many people assume casual sex happens after drinking, it's difficult to distinguish a guy's feelings about a girl who sleeps with him right away from a guy's feelings about a girl who "makes those types of decisions while drunk."

I don't think the idea of a slut is ever okay. But I do think it's important to recognize that "sluttiness" is not just about the act of sex; it's about having sex when that's not *really* what a girl wants to be doing. So a guy "not wanting to date a slut" ultimately boils down to wanting to date a girl who stands up for herself, is in control of her decisions, and respects her needs.

If you find yourself in a situation where you feel like a guy is looking down on you because you slept with him right away, you may want to explicitly tell him: "You didn't take advantage of me. I slept with you because I wanted to, not because I wasn't in control of my actions or didn't know what I was doing."

I want to feel special. Many guys said they were put off when a girl slept with them the night they met because it made them wonder, "How many other guys has she done this with?" One guy said, "If there's a reason to believe a girl had sex with you right away, but wouldn't do it with anyone else, then it's okay." Guys didn't want to be with a girl who was "easy" and would have sex with just anyone because, as one 25-year-old wrote: "That means I'm not special."

You want what other people don't have. It's a vain human thing that can come out in girls when we date bad boys. Something about the idea of being able to win over the impossible is appealing—like you must really be awesome if you can get a wild guy to change his ways.

Similarly, some guys just need to know your decision to have sex was about him (and his awesomeness). That you slept with him because you liked him, not because you would have done it with just anybody. Furthermore, some guys want to feel like they earned your affection. As one put it: "You fell for me when I was blackout drunk? You're not very bright." Guys want reassurance that not only do you like them, but also that you're not so indiscriminate you'd start liking just any guy you met. In some situations, you may want to tell a guy, "I think you're great, and I really like you. I wouldn't have gone home with just any guy I met."

After a one-night stand, I feel gross. No one is going to argue with the fact that sex feels good at the time. (Although, I guess for girls that's not always the case: "Sorry, dude, that's actually my pubic bone you're rubbing.") The real question is: How does it feel afterward? And the reality for many is that having sex with someone you don't know that well (and therefore can't like that much) can feel gross.

Said a 24-year-old at a mall in Seattle: "The morning after, I either feel good or awful. Good if you liked her and felt connected. But nights when you're drunk and just want to hook up, you feel bad because you just did it to relieve yourself." Another guy told me this: "Every time I've had a one-night stand I just want to sprint away. It just feels like a transaction." Sex is an intimate act, whether you like the person or not. And rubbing genitals with a stranger is just kinda gross, even for many guys.

Here's where it gets a bit tricky, though. As grossed out as many guys clearly are by casual sex, many will continue to do it because, as one said: "I'm a horny guy, and sex is still sex." This is all fine and good, except for the fact that instead of taking responsibility for their own gross horny actions, many guys simply transfer that "gross" feeling onto the girl. It's not "what happened was gross" or "I'm gross for doing it," it's "she's gross for having sex with me." It's easier to stomach that way, because then the grossness walks out the door with the one-night stand.

Even though many guys admitted that the morning after casual sex they feel a bit disgusted, very few made the connection that it was in their power to avoid it. It literally didn't occur to them that a girl could be willing to go all the way and they could say no—not because they weren't horny, but because they know they'll regret it the next day.

If you have sex with a guy too soon, you both wake up realizing it was a mistake, and he starts acting rudely—call him on it. Tell him, "Don't blame me for a mistake that we made. We shouldn't have had sex last night. But you are just as responsible for that decision as I am."

She doesn't want a relationship. The idea that a girl shouldn't sleep with a guy right away if she wants a relationship with him is one that's been ingrained in guys' heads as much as girls'. So much so, in fact, that some guys assume if you slept with them the first night, it's because you don't really like them. One guy from Boston told me: "If you meet someone, say three words to her, and then sleep together, you aren't looking for something and neither is she." Another guy said: "Times I've slept with a girl the first night, I haven't asked for her number, but she hasn't asked for mine either."

I met a good-looking 25-year-old who told me that while he would never think less of a girl who slept with him right away, he might worry about getting involved with her. "It's like this: If she does this all the time, is she going to want a relationship with me? Is she going to want to be monogamous?"

"Then it's threatening?" I asked.

"Yeah. That's a leading question, but I'd agree with you, yes. In the same way that a guy can be a player, if she did this with me so quickly, why would she not discard me and move on to someone else?"

Basically, sleeping with a guy right away may make him think you're not girlfriend material because you don't *want* to be a girlfriend. The fear is: If you're able to have sex "like a guy" (i.e., for the pleasure of it), then what would stop you from cheating? Would you really want to be monogamous? Could he trust you when you go out? Are you some kind of sex fiend? Really . . . all the same sort of insecurities that our culture has given us about men.

It's sort of damned if you do, damned if you don't. If you slept with a guy the night you met him and it wasn't what you really wanted, you risk losing respect. If you did it and it was what you wanted, then you risk losing trust.

So here is the cleanup: If you like a guy and sleep with him right away, the next morning do some damage control just in case (since you may not know his opinions about sex). Tell him: "I want you to know that I wouldn't have had sex with just anyone. I like you, and feel like I know you, so I thought it was the right thing to do."

How Soon Is "Too Soon"? And Will Having Sex Too Soon Literally Screw Me out of a Relationship?

Congrats. You made it past the first night. But now the question is: At what point in a dating relationship do you sleep with this guy? How soon is too soon?

"If you're dating a girl with the intention of possibly pursuing a relationship, at what point can you have sex with her without it negatively affecting your feelings about her?"

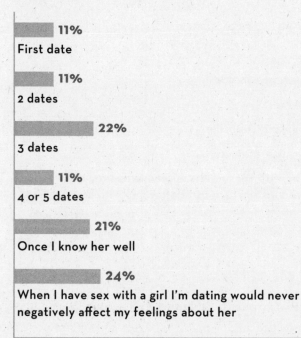

11%
First date

11%
2 dates

22%
3 dates

11%
4 or 5 dates

21%
Once I know her well

24%
When I have sex with a girl I'm dating would never negatively affect my feelings about her

0%   100%

And what if you miscalculate? Will sleeping with a guy "too soon" actually affect the future of your relationship?

"If you sleep with a girl 'too soon' (whatever too soon may be in your opinion), will it mess up the possibility of having a serious relationship with her?"

5%
No chance at all for a relationship

24%
A small chance for a relationship

31%
Some chance of a relationship

40%
When you sleep with her has absolutely no bearing on whether you end up in a serious relationship with her

0%   100%

Although there's no consensus about when "too soon" is, an interesting theme emerged among many responses. One guy wrote: "I can tell after two or three dates if we click, as soon as I get to the 'yes,' it is okay to sleep with her." And reiterated by another guy: "Once you make a connection, you can have sex without disrespect." And yet another one: "If she sleeps with me when I first meet her or on our first date, I probably haven't had enough time to take her seriously." Déjà vu of what many guys said about one-night stands: that sleeping with someone right away is okay only if you've truly made a connection. Also oddly reminiscent of what guys said about "the chase": that they want to be intimate with you emotionally before getting intimate physically. Could the fact that many guys are turned off when a girl sleeps with them "too soon" ultimately boil down to the reality that they actually want to know you before having sex? No! It couldn't be. Or could it?

These are just a handful of responses guys wrote about why having sex too soon can mess up the chances of a relationship:

"I want to know values and where that person is in their life before I even consider sleeping with someone."—29-year-old from Chicago

"You've gone 100% physically, maybe 20% emotionally, 40% trust and personality."—35-year-old from LA

"Building a foundation before sex is important."—24-year-old from Atlanta

Many guys want to get to know you before they sleep with you. Why? Because as one 24-year-old said: "I prefer having sex with girls I'm into." And if a guy doesn't really know you, how can he be into you? So if you're trying to figure out the ideal time to have sex with a guy you've been seeing, I would say wait until you've had a chance to really connect and understand each other. And if you really want a hard number here, wait at least three dates and you'll probably be in the clear.

The most important thing to consider, however, is when do YOU want to have sex? It takes two to tango, and it's not just about when the guy is okay with it, think about yourself too. Something we tend to forget as we get older and our number starts creeping up is that sleeping with a guy before you're really ready to can feel crappy. So yes, think about how sex will affect the relationship and what his reaction will be, but make sure you're also tuned in to how sex is going to affect number one.

Denver: "I Should Have Married Amy"

Apparently, asking strangers about their personal lives is technically soliciting. And because of this, while collecting surveys, I got kicked out of more places than I imagined possible. Too many bars to count, a handful of office courtyards, a Chipotle, and most impressively, I even got kicked out of a farmer's market.

For most places my strategy was to keep a low profile, and hand out surveys as discreetly as possible until someone noticed me and told me to leave. The exception was any small bar or coffee shop. In those places, I had no choice but to ask for permission because there was just no way to fly under the radar.

At a small bar/coffee shop in Denver, I had spoken with the manager, and even gotten permission to approach people sitting down at tables—a privilege that was entirely unheard of. Basking in the glory of getting to harass tables (not just guys standing by the bar), I spent the majority of the night nibbling on a vegan pizza with a group of four men, two of whom were married.

I asked all the married men the same questions: How did you know you wanted to get married? And how did you know she was the one? All of their answers were pretty much the same: We had been dating for a while, things worked, we were in love, had the same values, we were ready for a commitment, etc. All very legitimate answers, but honestly, all very boring. I didn't hear anything noteworthy until this night in Denver, when the quietest guy at the table opened up to tell this story:

"I had a long-term girlfriend I had been living with for a while. We had talked about marriage some, but I don't think it was a priority for either of us. I got really into outdoorsy stuff when I moved here, was a little cocky, and started doing things way above my skill level. I did this kayak trip that was way more difficult than anything I should have been doing. We had to go through a cave, and I got stuck. I was pinned in the cave under water. I thought I was going to die—I probably should have. It was one of those 'life flashing before your eyes' moments. And the thought that popped into my head when I was sure I was going to die was: 'I should have married Amy.'"

Caught off guard by the near-death experience, we were all stunned and silent. And then, we had to know why.

"I don't know. I think I just needed her to know that I wanted to give her that commitment. And I think that in return I needed to know she wanted to give that commitment to me."

A guy's dying thought, I should have gotten married? Not, I should have taken that trip to India, I should have jumped out of a plane, or I should have had a threesome. No, just simply: I should have married Amy.

Many scientists say that as humans we have a strong desire to pair-bond. And even though men are human, whenever we hear about their primal desires it almost always has to do with something sexual. We're told how everything from Internet porn to adultery is the result of a guy's drive to get some. But whether we commonly acknowledge it or not, men are also driven to commit to a life partner. So much so, that in what one guy thought were his dying moments, not solidifying that commitment was his biggest regret.

Does He Not Care Like I Do?

Are Guys Emotionally Affected By Relationships the Way Girls Are?

Relationships are tough. But they're made tougher by the fact that guys can seem like robots. As one of my best friends explains about her boyfriend: "I've learned that the blank stare he gets when we're in a fight is his form of crying." Her epiphany is brilliant—it's gotten me through many a blowout without completely losing my shit. There's just *nothing* more frustrating than being in a fight with your boyfriend, you're bawling your eyes out, and he's sitting there stone-faced. Then the fight escalates to "Don't you care?!? Aren't you upset?!?" Not that you're so callous as to want him to be in pain, but it would be nice for him to show some outward sign of emotion.

It can certainly seem like guys have the upper hand relationship-wise when they appear less affected by day-to-day relationship struggles. When we cry and they're stone-faced, it's infuriating, because it feels like they must be less emotionally invested in the relationship. But you can't always judge a book by its cover, because how guys are feeling on the inside isn't always reflected on the outside. A recent study found that men are actually more affected than women by strains in their romantic relationships.[1]

Guys may look like emotional robots, but that's not because they were born that way. Up until the age of one, baby boys are more emotionally expressive than baby girls—they cry more, they coo more, they smile more.[2] Then, between one and three, babies start learning about emotions.[3] A huge source of their learning is, of course, parents (specifically mothers) who spend more time talking about emotions with their daughters than they do talking about emotions with their sons.[4] And when mothers talk about feelings with their sons, they focus on anger, and react better when their sons respond to an upsetting situation by getting mad instead of sad.[5] You know, the whole "boys don't cry" bit.

Not surprisingly, by the age of four or five, little girls are more likely to talk about their feelings than little boys.[6] Boys in elementary school who cry in front of other kids are seen as wusses and are less popular than boys who suppress those feelings.[7] And this type of reinforcement that boys should not be emotional—unless they are getting pissed about something—continues throughout middle school, high school, and into adulthood. We basically take the emotionality that boys are born with, and we try to beat it out of them. We, as a culture, and yes, we as girls.

There's a great episode of the TV show *Louie* where the main character, played by Louis C.K., is on a date at a diner. Some roid-head high-school jock walks in and starts threatening him, saying he's going to kick his ass—a real threat since the kid's in great shape, while Louie is a chubby middle-aged man. The jock gives him an ultimatum: "Ask me nicely not to kick your ass or I'm going to do it." Making the mature decision not to get into a fight with a high schooler, Louie says: "Please don't kick my ass."

Afterward, his date tells him she doesn't want to see him again because giving in to the high-school bully was a turnoff. She says: "My mind is telling me you're a great guy, but my chemistry is telling me you're a loser." The sad reality is, a lot of girls aren't attracted to guys who act vulnerable. We tell guys—and show them—that in order to attract us they have to act macho and "manly." But then, once we're in a relationship, we're all "Why don't you ever cry or show any emotion?" The messages we send men about how we want them to act can be both confusing and contradictory.

But as much as we knowingly and unknowingly encourage men to hide their feelings, those feelings are still there. In a study designed to look at male and female differences in emotion, men and women were shown movie clips that were happy, sad, or scary. While watching these clips, they were observed as well as hooked up to devices that measured physical signs of emotion. When viewing the clips, women's faces showed significantly greater reactions. But when asked about how they felt, men and women had similar reports. And the devices that measured the physical responses to emotion actually found greater reactions in men.[8] Obviously this study is not a perfect match for real-world scenarios, but it does indicate that—crazily enough—guys actually feel things. It also shows that guys' inner feelings aren't always on display, hence the "I'm bawling and my boyfriend is staring at me blankly" scenario.

The implication of men's pesky emotions is that, romantically speaking, guys have emotional needs as well as sexual ones. Just like us, guys want their significant others to provide them with lots of warmth and affection.[9] Even if they don't talk about it as openly, when we're not being affectionate, guys feel hurt, neglected, and taken for granted. When we act distant, it makes them feel insecure. When we're not supportive and encouraging, it makes them feel like we don't think they're important. If you've ever caught yourself thinking, "Oh, he won't care that I blah-blah-blah, he's a guy," think again.

"Guys may not call a girl on the little things," said a guy from San Francisco. "But when your girlfriend doesn't call when she says she will, or doesn't text you back, it makes you ask questions. Those little things affect guys the same way they affect girls." Guys get just as hurt, offended, and upset in relationships (both casual and serious) as girls do. So if you're wondering what might hurt or upset him, analyze if that action would hurt or upset you.

Am I His Priority, or Does He Care More About "the Fellas"?

People like to give advice. Drunk people LOVE to give advice. Fresh out of college and working at a bar, I got this nugget from a tipsy 40-something woman and her friend: "Never marry a guy who doesn't have hobbies and friends. If he doesn't have his own thing going on, he's gonna be too needy and he's gonna drive you crazy." I love this advice because I think it's so true—but it's something that can be easy to lose sight of the times when you feel like a guy is constantly choosing to hang out with his friends instead of you.

Times like that, instead of feeling lucky to be with a guy who has a life, you feel abandoned by a guy who seems to always have priorities other than your relationship.

The question is: Can we ever expect to be a guy's priority, or is it just a sad truth that relationships are a girl thing? Judging by beer commercials, guys just want to grab a cold one and hang out with their dude bros. Their girlfriends are just somewhere on the sidelines, pouting about the fact that they can't hold their boyfriends' attention as well as a crappy light beer. But what do real guys say? Are you his priority? Or is he indeed more concerned with his buddies?

"Who comes first? Your girlfriend or the guys?"

24%
Girlfriend all the way

34%
Girlfriend by a hair

28%
It's a tie

9%
Guys by a hair

4%
Guys all the way

0%   100%

Despite what advertising executives think about intimate relationships, 86% of guys say their girlfriends are just as much of a priority as their guy friends (if not more). And when you look at guys who answered this question who are actually *in* relationships, they're even more dedicated to their girlfriends. This is the breakdown between guys who are in serious relationships and guys who aren't:

"Who comes first? Your girlfriend or the guys?"

Girlfriend all the way
- 36%
- 23%

Girlfriend by a hair
- 40%
- 34%

It's a tie
- 20%
- 29%

Guys by a hair
- 2%
- 10%

Guys all the way
- 2%
- 4%

0%   100%

■ SERIOUS RELATIONSHIP
■ OTHER GUYS

You are your boyfriend's priority. Once guys are actually in serious relationships, three out of four put their girlfriends first. Almost all the rest say their girlfriend is as much of a priority as their guy friends, except for a tiny 4% of guys who are still more concerned with "the fellas." So in reality, that beer commercial image only exists 4% of the time.

The catch here is this: Just because you are your boyfriend's priority, it doesn't mean that you will always feel like it. That's at least in part because everyone's relationship expectations are different. A 27-year-old told me that a huge source of contention in a past long-distance relationship was talking on the phone. His girlfriend wanted to talk for a long time every day. He didn't like talking on the phone and thought chatting every few days would be fine. Now, judging from his actions, you might assume he was less into the relationship than she was (since he wanted less contact). But, he later went on to tell me he always felt like he loved her more than she loved him. In his mind, the fact that he had priorities that came before their phone calls (i.e., hanging out with his friends) had absolutely *nothing* to do with how much he cared about her. Of course, she probably thought it did, otherwise she wouldn't have been so adamant about wanting to talk every day. What your boyfriend's actions mean to you may not be what his actions mean to him. And while you might take something as a sign he's less dedicated to the relationship than you are, he may not see it that way at all.

Your boyfriend having a life outside of you does not mean that he's not into your relationship or that he doesn't care about you that much. You may be *a* priority, but he'll still have other priorities as well: wanting to hang out with his friends, needing to spend a lot of time at work, or pursuing interests of his that don't involve you—and that's what a healthy relationship *should* look like. A 30-year-old in Seattle told me (and many other guys had similar thoughts): "You need to have your own life outside of your relationship. I feel like sometimes girls don't get that, and they get pissed when you go out with your guy friends. They think you're going out to meet girls or something, and that's not it at all. You just want to hang out with your friends."

Will your boyfriend choose to do things other than hang out with you? Yes. But that's a good thing. Because like the woman in the bar said: You wouldn't want to be with a guy who's attached to your hip all the time.

If your boyfriend never puts you first, that's one thing. But making time for things other than you is not a sign he cares about you any less than you care about him. If the way he's acting is making you question his dedication, tell him. Perhaps if he made his affection more clear in other ways, you wouldn't be as hurt by his smaller everyday actions. Relationships are all about making compromises. If what you really want is a greater demonstration of your boyfriend's devotion, it's very possible he can give you that in ways that don't involve him doing something he doesn't want to do (like talking on the phone for hours or giving up guys' night).

We've Been Dating for Months. Why Isn't He Saying "I Love You"?

Getting to the bottom of men's thoughts about love led to the most confusing and roundabout question on the survey. When I'd hand out the questionnaire, I'd warn guys: "I know Question 33 is ridiculous. Feel free not to answer it." I figured that maybe 100 guys would take the time to write in an answer, and that perhaps some of their thoughts would be useful. I did not expect that the majority of guys would take the time to answer the question or that I'd be receiving hundreds of mini essays about love. (I also wasn't thinking about what a pain in the ass it was going to be to type them all up.)

This is the question I asked: "You and your girlfriend have been seriously dating for a while, you both have deep feelings for each other, but you haven't said 'I love you.' Do you love her? And if so, why haven't you told her? If not, what is the difference between the feelings you have for her and love?" Even though the question was open-ended and had many parts, most answers fell into the same few categories.

2%
I'm emotionally damaged

34%
I'm scared to tell her/want her to say it first

28%
Love is a big commitment

5%
I'm waiting for the right time

12%
I'm not sure yet

18%
I don't love her

0%   100%

Emotionally damaged. Guys in this category explicitly said they were emotionally damaged, wrote they didn't believe in love, or made clear they had some other issue. One said: "I don't even say that to my mother . . . whom I do love."

I'm scared to tell her/want her to say it first. Though many guys will be quick to talk about girls being so eager to have relationships and make commitments, on some level they must not completely believe their own words. Or at least once they've fallen for a girl they start to question them. About a third of guys (34%) aren't telling their girlfriends they love them because they don't want to "freak her out," ruin the relationship, or have their feelings go unreturned.

A 45-year-old from LA wrote: "I'm afraid to say 'I love you' because girls generally fear a guy who comes on too strong. Being honest and overly affectionate is not successful." A 22-year-old from Chicago said: "Most guys don't tell a girl they love her because they feel like they may ruin the mystery, thereby making the girl feel like she could walk away."

Of course, part of wanting the girl to say "I love you" first was no doubt to save face in case the feelings were not returned. As a 27-year-old admitted: "I always let her say it first because I am a pussy." A guy in Houston felt this way: "The girl should always say it first so that I'm not in the awkward position of waiting for her to say it back. I might love the girl, but I'm not going to tell her until she tells me." One guy from New York even thought: "Saying 'I love you' first is emasculating."

Love is a big commitment. Call me a love whore, but I guess the words *I love you* have never had the connotation of long-term commitment to me. I see it as "I have really strong feelings for you. I care about your well-being like you were family, and I'm completely dedicated to this relationship." It's not a promise of "I will feel this way forever." It's not an engagement, it says nothing about the intention of marriage, and it's not signed in blood. I can't say for sure that the majority of girls see it this way also, but I can say that many guys don't. For at least 28% of guys, the words *I love you* mean much, much more.

One 31-year-old wrote: "'I love you' has become heavily weighted. 'I love you' leads to engagement, which leads to marriage. It is not a phrase to be taken lightly." A 29-year-old from Chicago wrote: "Love is for life and based on commitment, not feelings." A 26-year-old added: "Love seems more final; if you love her you should be talking marriage at some point." And a 23-year-old even went as far as to say: "Love means you'd die for her."

For many guys it's clear that love is a promise as well as a feeling. So it's no wonder some guys can be so gun-shy about saying "I love you." Many of them see it as a phrase that sets off a chain reaction to a deeper—possibly lifelong—commitment. One guy even said, "I may not tell a girl I love her if I don't think the relationship is going to be long-term and possibly end in marriage."

If you've been with a guy for a while and it's starting to get serious, don't worry if he's not dropping L-bombs. There's a good chance that he's waiting on you to say it first. So if you're ready to take the relationship there, here's your green light to do it. There's also a good chance that he takes the phrase *very* seriously and is just giving the relationship more time to develop. The fact that he isn't saying "I love you" is not by any means a sign that he doesn't care about you or that the relationship isn't going anywhere.

Is He Terrified of Marriage?
And Will He Ever Be Ready?

We're told that wanting to get married is a "girl thing" and a ball and chain that guys want to avoid at all costs. But one thing that blew my mind constantly while interviewing guys is how many of them would slip in comments about "the one," marriage, or their "future wife."

When I asked a 26-year-old if sleeping with a girl right away would mess up the chances of a relationship: "It could. But if I met 'the one,' I don't think that it would matter."

In a conversation about life after college with a 24-year-old:

Him: "After I graduated I moved out to Jackson Hole for six months to be a ski bum."

Me: "That's awesome. Did you make friends and stuff, or were you mostly alone?"

Him: "I mean, you're not meeting your future wife, but yeah, there are definitely people around."

Listening to the random yakking of a male acquaintance:

"I want them to play 'Another One Bites the Dust' at my wedding." This was followed by two more wedding-related comments in the following weeks.

Seriously, guys are obsessed with getting married. They can't stop talking about it! I cannot tell you how many times "the future wife" and "the one" were mentioned in conversations that were about sex, casual dating, or even something else entirely. Sure, some guys may bring up marriage in a negative context to avoid ridicule, but it's clearly something that's on the forefront of their minds.

A full 95% of the guys I interviewed said they'd like to get married someday. For good reason too: Married men are physically and mentally healthier, and they live longer than men who are single.[10] Studies also show that men are actually happier in their marriages than women.[11] And when a guy gets divorced or his wife dies, he's faster to remarry than a woman in the same position.[12] Not only do guys want to get married, they're happier and healthier after they do it, and if something happens to their marriage, they're chomping at the bit to do it again.

Guys don't want to wait forever to get married either. On average, the ones in my survey wanted to seal the deal by 32½. Breaking it down a bit by age (since a 33-year-old who wanted to get married couldn't write anything under 33), the average age guys under 27 wanted to get married by was 30, and the average age guys 27 and older wanted to get married by was 35. The "biological clock" isn't just a female thing. Sure, technically guys can settle down and pop out some kids when they're 80, but most don't want to. Maybe the biological pressure isn't quite as tough on men, but for many, a self-imposed clock ticks just as loudly.

A number of guys didn't have an exact age they wanted to be married by, but instead wanted to have reached some personal milestones. The milestone guys talked about the most had to do with their finances.

As a girl, most of us can't fully relate to the pressure to be financially successful (or at the very least stable). Politically correct or not, we're just not expected to be able to single-handedly support a family or be the primary breadwinner. If you have a job that pays well, that's great. But if you don't, you're not neglecting your wifely duties. One guy I surveyed actually wrote that his biggest relationship concern was "not having/making enough money to be a responsible boyfriend or spouse." And a guy in San Francisco told me: "There's a financial expectation to have what your parents have or surpass it. Once you have that in place, then you can think about starting a family." A guy wanting to sort out his finances before getting married is not some commitment-delaying excuse; it's a legitimate concern for many guys.

Along with their financials being in place, guys obviously want to be in a stable relationship before they commit as well. If a guy and his girlfriend are arguing a lot and still trying to assess their compatibility, he (understandably) isn't going to want to take that next step. A 28-year-old who's been with his girlfriend nine months told me this: "If you're going to get engaged, then things have to be working out. If you're having a lot of questions and you're having to give your girlfriend the benefit of the doubt all the time, then it's not a good idea to get married. Before you get married you have to know for sure that the relationship works." A 32-year-old in a two-year relationship added: "You know you've found the right girl when it doesn't feel like work. It should be easy. The responsibilities you have in a relationship need to feel natural, and not like a chore."

If you and your boyfriend are struggling to get along, and still assessing whether or not your life visions are in line, don't be surprised if he's not popping the question (in fact, be relieved . . . that's not the kind of relationship you should commit to either). In order for a guy to start thinking about tying the knot, he has to feel stable and secure in both his finances and in his relationship.

What Makes My Boyfriend Question Our Relationship, and Is He Hiding Any Dirty Secrets from Me?

As if we needed proof that all relationships are different, on the original survey I asked guys, "What about your girlfriend or your relationship makes you question your relationship the most?" I got 12 pages of different answers. Can I tell you what your boyfriend's biggest relationship concern is? No, not at all. (Although, judging from the many responses, he probably can, so you may want to ask him.) What I *can* tell you are the major issues that make guys question their relationships, and perhaps it will help you navigate your own.

The majority of guys' relationship concerns boil down to three categories. The first one is trust. Can he trust your commitment to the relationship? Can he trust you're as emotionally invested as he is? Can he trust that you believe in him? A 24-year-old questioned "whether my girlfriend truly supports me and has faith in our relationship and me as a man." And a 29-year-old worried about his girlfriend's "willingness to let me in completely."

Guys also questioned if they could trust their girlfriends' faithfulness, which was called into question mainly because of flirty behavior, excessive nights out, and exes. One guy was skeptical of "the time my girlfriend spends at clubs with her friends," while another one worried about "the way she interacts with other men." Stereotypically, we think of guys as the ones who cheat. But guys don't trust us that much either. When I asked guys who they thought cheated more, guys or girls, 27% said guys, 11% said girls, and 62% thought both cheat the same amount. (It should be clear by now what guys think about their own sexual conduct, so thinking we're as likely to cheat as they are cannot be good.)

Guys worry about committing to a girl who's sketchy. So if there's any part of you that thinks flirting with other guys or being emotionally unavailable is going to make him more interested, nip that thought in the bud, because it won't. All it will make him do is question your relationship more.

The second category many guys wrote about was "Is she really the one?" Guys question what will happen in the future, whether the relationship can last, and as one wrote: "Can I really be around this person all the time for the rest of my life?" Although a few guys were worried about their ability to commit and remain monogamous, many more cited compatibility concerns: "The amount of fun we have." "The lack of mutual interests/compatibility as I get to know her." "How often we fight." "Problems communicating. Knowing she trusts me and tells me when I hurt her feelings, caring when she hurts mine." Guys were also worried about differences in age, religion, life goals, and values.

Finally, there were the individual complaints about the girls themselves. Guys were not fans of their girlfriends acting clingy, codependent, and "overly emotional." A 24-year-old was bothered by his girlfriend "not being able to understand my needs: personal time and friend time." And a 30-year-old complained about his girlfriend "being too needy."

Guys don't want a girlfriend who's codependent, but there's clearly a balance to strike, because they don't want us to be completely emotionally uninvested either. A 37-year-old wrote that he questioned his relationship the most at times when "she's more absorbed in her own things than us." And many of the trust concerns just mentioned centered around a girl's commitment and investment in the relationship. So while guys don't want their girl-friends to be overly clingy, they still want them to be affectionate and show clear dedication. Luckily, investing time and energy into your relationship while at the same time maintaining your own life is a recipe to keep both *you* and him happy.

Another thing that drove guys up the wall was when their girl-friends were naggy, insecure, and controlling. And I get it, acting this way is annoying, but give us a break. All we've heard our whole lives is how assholey guys are, so is it really any wonder we can get overly suspicious about what our boyfriends do? But for any of you reading this who might have slightly controlling tendencies (no judgments, we've all been there), it might be help-ful to know that guys are pretty honest in relationships.

When I asked guys if there was anything specific they were hiding from their girlfriends or lying to them about, 86% said no. The 14% of guys who said yes mentioned past skeletons in their closets or general unsavory traits, such as drinking, smoking, lazi-ness, debt, dorky friends, and my personal favorite answer to this question: video games. That's right, there are guys out there who aren't telling you they own an Xbox and spend some Saturdays on their headsets talking smack to 12-year-olds.

There were a handful of guys who were hiding cheating (both physical and emotional) and feelings they still have for their exes. But this handful was small, and by no means representative of most boyfriends. Yes, there are guys who cheat. But it's not the majority, and you can't let the few bad seeds make you so crazy that it ruins your relationship with a good one.

As long as your boyfriend has given you no reason to distrust him, ignore whatever part of you is saying, "Be skeptical because he's a guy." A guy said to me once: "My girlfriend is constantly accusing me of cheating on her or hitting on other girls when I go out with my friends. I'm not like that at all, but at this point I feel like I may as well be, because no matter how good I am she's going to be yelling at me and accusing me anyway." If you can't trust a guy, dump him. If you can trust him, you just have to let go of your anxieties. When you don't, and you let them make you insecure and controlling, it just pushes him away.

The vast majority of the things that make guys question their relationships are not too different from the things that would raise our eyebrows. They're skeptical of being involved with a girl they can't trust, who has no life of her own, is emotionally unstable, and places too many restrictions on what they can and cannot do. More than that, they worry about compatibility, communication issues, and whether or not it's a good fit. Many also look to the future and wonder, can I really see this relationship going the distance?

Is My Boyfriend Watching Porn Because He Wants Other Girls?

It used to be that the "kind of guy who watched porn" was somewhat sketchy. To get it, a guy had to pay—literally and figuratively. He had to go into the private section of the video store, deal with the embarrassment of checking it out at the counter, and then sheepishly return it five days later. He needed to be pretty motivated to get his hands on those dirty videos because it required a decent amount of effort. Now, the "kind of guy who watches porn" is pretty much anyone with a laptop. The Internet has made it more accessible, more private, and more mainstream.

It's probably not all that shocking to you that guys watch porn. But what can be surprising, and even hurtful, is the fact that many still watch porn when they're in relationships. Why? If you're getting laid regularly, why the triple X?

Of the guys I surveyed, 77% said they still watched porn when they had a girlfriend. For the most part, the ones who didn't said it was because they weren't porn men to begin with—it didn't have anything to do with the fact that they were in relationships. As one said: "I haven't ever; it's dumb." The majority who continued to watch porn when they had a girlfriend explained themselves like this 29-year-old from Denver: "Porn is masturbating and masturbating is normal."

You might worry that your boyfriend's porn habit is about his dissatisfaction with you, or his desire to fantasize about other women. But it's about jerking off. And guys jerk off to porn because watching people have sex is arousing. Why do guys in relationships want to jerk off? Because, as a 27-year-old put it: it's "different than sex with my girlfriend. It's pure quick-release." In a discussion about watching porn while in a committed relationship, a young Ph.D. candidate explained: "Whenever I have sex with my girlfriend, I'm so busy thinking about her, putting pressure on myself to last longer, be a good lover, and whatever. Sometimes it's a relief just to jack off and not have to be thinking about someone else."

Our bodies are complicated. To get us to the big O (or at least in that direction), guys really have to work for it: get hard, stay hard, don't cum too fast, use your hands dumbass, no, not there, there! Sometimes guys (and all people, really) just want to get off quickly and easily. Besides, logistically speaking, there will likely be times when your boyfriend is horny and you're not around.

And in that case, you guessed it, porn time—or as one guy said: "relaxation and stress relief whenever I want it."

There were a *few* guys who described their porn habit as "I get tired of the same girl," and wrote about liking porn because they wanted to look at the women. But the overwhelming majority of guys saw it as simply a means to an end, a tool that (much like a vibrator) made masturbation easier. I don't know how much porn you've seen, but the majority of the stars aren't exactly supermodels. If watching porn were just about drooling over hot girls, it would make more sense to jerk off to a Victoria's Secret catalog.

Not only do many guys with girlfriends still watch porn, a decent number mentioned watching porn *with* their girlfriends. Although we tend to think of porn as "a guy thing," studies show women find it arousing too.[13]

If you're having trouble understanding why your man watches nudie flicks, maybe you should try watching some. You can even find videos that are specifically made for women. And better yet, lots of the sites online are free. (I'm sure you can ask your boyfriend for a good recommendation if you're having trouble finding one.)

A guy watching porn is only a problem if he's neglecting your sexual needs because he's too busy jerking himself off. Many guys wrote that they opted for porn when sex with their girlfriends wasn't an option. If sex with you is an option but he's regularly choosing to spend time with his laptop instead, then it's time to confront him about his habit. Otherwise, it's nothing to be concerned about. It doesn't mean he wants other girls or that you're not hot enough. It just means that he feels like masturbating. Which is everyone's right, in or out of a relationship.

CASE STUDY: ZACK

Zack's one of those guys who's just effortlessly cool. I don't even think he showers much, and he doesn't dress well, but he exudes such warmth and is so interesting you can't help but be drawn to him. No doubt about it, he's a heartbreaker. And you'd hate him for it, but he's just too lovable.

The thing about Zack is he's got a lot of love and a lot of excitement. So when girls start dating him, they fall quickly. And he does too, but then he seems to fall out of it just as fast—like a kid who one week is obsessed with being a skateboarder and the next is on to something else. By his own account, he's "fallen in love with a good number of women, but not sure [he's] ever been in love."

When I first started following Zack's love life he was 27, had just met a girl he was falling in love with, and was about to relocate to a different city. About his new girl he said, "I'm completely falling for her. I think about having a future with her and it doesn't even scare me! I'm so giddy about it, I can't believe myself." This was a month into the relationship, and about a month before it became long distance.

Three months later, the relationship was crumbling. He no longer felt attached or connected to her, and was surprised to find himself starting to be attracted to other girls. A month after that, it was over.

It's one thing to be ditched by a guy who acted moderately interested the whole time. But it's quite another to be ditched by a guy after things start off so intensely. Many girls have been there. Where one second a guy is falling in love with you, and then a few quick months later it's "on to the next one." When this happens, what the hell went wrong?

When Zack told me about his breakup, I wanted to be sympathetic, but honestly, I felt for the girl. Appropriate or not, I had to push him: "I'm sorry you're going through this, and I'm not trying to be a dick here . . . but how is something over so quickly when a few months ago you were head over heels? I mean, you were obsessed with this girl. I can flip back in my journal and read you some quotes if you want . . ."

He defended himself. "You see, I got swept up in the feeling, as opposed to actually thinking about compatibility. It's easy to get caught up in the feeling of being in love and not be thoughtful about it being a good match. But at some point that feeling levels out, and then if it's not perfect compatibility, you feel it. In some ways it was the distance, because when you're caught up doing stuff together, you don't have a sense of what someone does in their free time, who they really are, or what their hobbies are. When you don't know a person that well, you fill in the blanks with perfection. But then once you know more, you wonder: Was she doing things I liked for me? To impress me? Or do we actually have the same interests? It seemed like a lot of the things I had fallen in love with weren't actually her. And once I knew her better, I realized we weren't actually compatible."

For as much hell as I was ready to give him, he made some really decent points. There's compatible in person and compatible on paper. And they're both important. In-person compatibility is the chemistry, and that's obvious right away; that's the love at first sight. Are you attracted to each other? Do you click? Do you enjoy being in each other's presence? Can you have good conversations? Do you make each other laugh?

And then, there's compatibility on paper. Do you have the same values? Interests? Do you make the kinds of life choices that the other person can respect? If you were both on eHarmony, would your profiles have a high matching percentage?

The problem with falling in love with someone quickly is that you're not really falling in love with them; you're falling in love with how they present themselves and who you think they might be. At some point, those initial fireworks die down, you get to know the person better, and you see the person for who he or she truly is. And at that point, your true compatibility can't be ignored.

A guy I met at The Grove in LA wrote a three-paragraph essay on the back of his survey. This is part of it: "I used to think I was into building something with a girl slowly, but then felt I was more of the 'thunderbolt' type, where passion just hits you and if it's 'real' you go from there. Such an outlook also leads to impatience and can overvalue emotions against reason."

Falling in love feels good. And to the extent that we're all just rats wanting to push down on the pedal that administers some sort of pleasure, sometimes we just let ourselves fall—even when we're doing it blindly. And then, people get hurt.

Next time you meet a guy and it starts out with a bang, enjoy it. But keep in perspective what it really is. It can take only a second to fall in love. But the quicker you fall into love, the quicker you can fall out of it, because it's not based on anything substantial. So while you should always get excited about meeting a guy that you click with in person, know that the next test is whether or not you click on paper.

Atlanta: The Breakup

Twenty-four hours into my trip and I was curled up on the corner of my hotel couch sobbing. That embarrassing guttural type of crying where it's unclear if the culprit is someone giving birth, a whiny lap dog, or a girl with really obnoxious sex noises.

Twelve hours earlier, I had delivered this speech to my boyfriend: "I want to have a great boyfriend, just a really good guy who's going to go out of his way for me, and for my friends. That's the kind of boyfriend I want, eventually the kind of husband I want, and the kind of father I want for my kids. If that's never going to be you, that's okay. But then you have to let me go find the guy who is."

You never give those types of ultimatums thinking you're actually going to hear, "You're right, I'm going to get out of your way." And had I known that was going to be the outcome, I probably would have chosen my words more carefully. But after two years of "I know I take you for granted," I was sick of settling. And I had met too many wonderful guys on my trips to think that settling was an option.

I'm what you might call an impatient reader. When I start a book, I flip to the last page before I've even finished the first chapter. And cynical as it is, when I start a relationship, I always imagine how the breakup is going to go down. But with this one, I had actually thought that maybe it wouldn't. So I guess that's how things end with a guy you think you might marry. Unexpectedly, accidentally, and over the phone. The worst part is, I couldn't even wallow in my own misery. I had to get out there and collect surveys. Hit the streets of Atlanta in my rented bright yellow Beetle—a ridiculous car to be driving around when you're in a state of depression.

Sadness comes in waves. I suppose it's your body's half-assed attempt at self-preservation. I had thought I could keep it together and was in the Highlands having guys fill out surveys when it came creeping back. Like that feeling right before you puke, when you can literally feel it rising up through your entire body. It was one of the few times in my life when the words going through my head were, "I'm not okay." I sat down on a bench to collect myself but then saw the road sign across the street was my ex-boyfriend's name. You've got to be kidding me.

Feeling like I could die right then and there, I dug for my phone and tried every one of my friends who knew what was going on. No answer. That's when he rode up to me on his bike, a guy I had just given the survey to, and apparently smiled at.

"So if you're in Atlanta for a while and don't know anyone, I was hoping I could take you out for dinner."

I burst into tears. His friend across the street shot him a look like, "What the hell did you say to this girl?" My very rehearsed "I have a boyfriend" answer was no longer necessary, and that realization shocked me. The poor guy looked utterly confused.

"I'm so sorry. I just broke up with my boyfriend three hours ago, and I wasn't expecting to have to deal with a question like that."

"Oh." He paused. "Well, I'd still love to take you to dinner or something if you're up for it."

"That's very sweet of you, but honestly, I can't promise that I wouldn't be crying the entire time."

He reached out, put his hand on my arm, looked into my eyes, and said, "If you were, I think I could handle it."

It was the most gentlemanly thing a guy had done for me in a long time, and we agreed to meet for a drink the following night. He texted the next day to see if I wanted him to pick me up at my hotel, what kind of bar I wanted to go to, and if there was anywhere in Atlanta I wanted to see. He took me to a bar with a beautiful view of the city and we had a beer and talked about life, love, and dating. We decided to meet up the next night as well when I was done collecting surveys. The second night, we walked around Midtown admiring the buildings, and then drove around some fancy neighborhood looking at mansions.

He was a perfect southern gentleman. The kind of guy that resets your mind, "Oh, right. This is how you're supposed to be treated." No, I didn't kiss him. And yes, he was attractive. But we were very different people with very different goals, and I didn't want to lead him on that there was even a slight possibility of sparking up an interstate romance. Along with not kissing him, I made sure to drop a lot of F-bombs so he'd realize that I didn't fit the mold of the "sweet southern wife" he was looking for anyway.

When I got back to my hotel the last night we hung out, he sent me this text: "Rather than spit out directions when saying good-bye, what I'd like to have said was that I am lucky to have met you, that you are inspiring and good-hearted. I hope I am lucky enough to meet you again."

I can't explain exactly why, but hanging out with him got me through those first few days of the breakup. I hope it's not for a reason as pathetic as I needed attention from a guy to feel better—though in all honesty I'm sure that played a part. But more than that, it was having comfort and companionship when dealing with one of the most emotional moments of my life, with all of my loved ones hundreds of miles away.

A few years ago, I went to a psychic who told me there was a guardian angel looking over me. (I know, psychic, guardian angel? Look, I'm an atheist. I don't have God, you gotta give me something.) After wrestling around with who it might be, I settled on Richard, my mom's brother who died in a car accident when he was seventeen. I never met him, but I've seen quite a few pictures, and out of everyone on both sides of my family, he is the person I look the most like. For the past few years I've felt that he is my own personal deity.

As you may have just guessed, the man I met in Atlanta is also named Richard. Coincidence? Possibly. But I'd like to believe that my guardian sent a messenger to help me through a difficult few days.

After leaving Atlanta, I heard from Richard one last time, a week and a half after I left, on my particularly difficult 27th birthday. I hadn't told him my birthday was coming, and he had no idea. My phone beeped with a text. Richard Atlanta: "Saw a flashy yellow Beetle on the road. All right now, Amber . . . keep on keeping on."

If I do have a guardian angel, and this was a sign, here is what it meant: It's hard to give up the stability and comfort of a relationship. But you can't settle for a guy who takes you for granted. Even though right now it feels like you're all alone, you're not. The good ones are out there. Waiting. And when you take a leap of faith to find one, you will be rewarded.

Is His Sexuality More Complex Than "Pork It"?

GUYS AND SEX

Are Guys Controlled by Their Penises?

The legend of men's horniness reaches epic proportions, from the 5,000 times a day they supposedly think about sex, to who they'd be willing to bang, to exactly how immoral they will be in order to get laid. Somehow, we have bought into this idea that when a six-foot-tall man is up against his six-inch-long dick, his dick will win. And because men are *so* incredibly, undeniably, clothes-ripping-off horny, how can we expect them to contain their urges? When it comes to sex, anything is fair game, because what did you expect? He is, after all, a guy.

But is any of this true? Are guys actually controlled by their penises? Are they uncontrollably horny in ways that women just are not?

It defies common logic, but men and women aren't *that* different when it comes to sex. A 2010 meta-analysis comparing men and women's sexuality looked at the results of studies published from 1993 to 2007 as well as statistics on sexual behavior, and found pretty unspectacular differences. On the whole, guys reported slightly more sexual activity than girls, and slightly more "permissive" sexual attitudes (basically, guys are more likely to think sex in a certain situation is okay). There were slightly larger differences between the amount that men and women said they masturbated, watched porn, and engaged in casual sex. (Guys reported doing all of these things more often.)[1]

Though some differences do exist between men and women's sexuality, they are not large. Even a "medium-sized difference"—like the one found between the amount of casual sex that men and women have engaged in—would still mean that almost a third of women have had more casual sex than the average man. And a "small difference"—like number of partners reported—means that 42% of women have had more partners than the average guy. Even where there are *statistically* significant differences between men and women's sexuality, there is still a huge amount of overlap from one group to the other. It's not like men are one way sexually and women are the complete opposite. Something that produces a "significant" difference, scientifically speaking, may not actually be all that significant in the real world

Chances are, even the small differences that do exist may be explained—at least in part—by our cultural expectations. Girls say they masturbate less than guys. Is that because they're less horny? Or because the idea of a masturbating guy is more culturally acceptable than a masturbating girl? Girls report having less casual sex. Again, is that because they want sex less, or because it's less "okay" for them to be having sex outside of a relationship? *Or,* are girls and guys actually having the *same* amount of casual sex, but fudging their numbers a bit to give answers that "sound good." How does that saying go? When a guy tells you his number, divide it by three; and when a girl gives you her number, multiply it by three.

A major problem with studying sexuality is that much of the data is based on self-reporting. And since sex is such an emotionally charged issue, can we expect people to be completely honest about their experiences?

A study set up to test this problem asked college students how many people they had slept with under three different conditions: in an anonymous survey, when they were hooked up to a (fake) lie detector (so assumed they had to tell the truth), and when they had to turn in their questionnaire to another student. When hooked up to a "lie detector," guys and girls reported almost identical numbers; when answering anonymously, guys reported more partners than girls, and when turning in answers to a peer, the gap between guys' and girls' numbers got even bigger.[2]

The slight differences that have been measured between men's and women's sexuality likely have as much to do with gender standards as innate differences in horndogness. This means that men are controlled by their penises to the same extent that women are controlled by their vaginas. Or, if gender standards aren't responsible for the differences, men are controlled by their genitals 5% to 10% more. So imagine you were 10% more horny. Would you be unable to make rational decisions? No, of course not. And this means that, shockingly, men are actually in control of their penises, and not vice versa.

Does Sex Fulfill Every Male Need?

At a café in Denver, a guy completing the survey approached me as soon as he was done answering the questions.

"You really want to know about guys and sex?" He spoke in a hushed tone and looked around worriedly, like he was a snitch and I was an FBI agent.

"Yeah, I *really* want to know. That's why I'm here."

"Well, I'm involved in the adult film industry. I direct."

Now he had my interest. "Oh? Well, what can you tell me about guys and sex . . . as a guy who directs porn."

"Believe it or not, the guys who get into porn are nice guys. They mean well and are just looking for something hedonistic. They have this 'what if I die tomorrow' mentality. They get into porn thinking they're living out a fantasy. But then they don't end up very happy."

"How come?"

"I think part of it is that they can't lead a normal life outside of what they do because they're so private about it. They can't have normal relationships. So they end up in these open relationships with other adult film stars. And then they get messed up. I mean, I've been in the industry 15 years and known three guys who've killed themselves. The suicide rate in the industry is much higher in men than women. I don't know any of the girls who have killed themselves."

"Well, why do you think that is?" I had to keep prompting him so that he would continue talking—kinda like feeding a parking meter.

"Oh, for one, it's easier for the women to have an outside life. There's just a double standard, and they seem to have an easier time finding a boyfriend who can deal with their lifestyle. I guess there just aren't that many girls out there who will seriously date a male porn star. So the guys just get lonely, maybe. I don't know."

Here you have the stereotypical male fantasy: sleeping with hundreds of women (and getting paid for it!), and many of the men who actually live it end up depressed. So depressed that some even decide to end their lives. Why? As speculated by this director: their profession is preventing them from having meaningful intimate relationships. Despite the jokes many guys will so readily make about wanting sex above all else, the truth is, being able to have sex but not relationships wouldn't actually make them happy.

And yet, this idea that getting laid is the golden key to men's happiness is one that's alive and well. So alive, there are some guys who actually believe it, and live their lives accordingly. And as one researcher on masculinity put it: "For guys like that you just have to ask, 'Oh yeah, buddy? How's that workin' out for ya?'" If this porn star anecdote is any indication, probably not too well.

Sex isn't actually guys' top need or priority. This means that simply having sex with a guy is not the only thing you have to do to keep him happy (and it's certainly not the way to get him interested). As discussed in the previous chapter, guys have needs that are emotional as well as physical. One guy told me: "At 22 I wasn't ready to settle down. But I still wanted more than just sex."

Do Guys Want Sex ALL of the Time?

Just like sex isn't the be-all and end-all to male fulfillment, it's also not something guys actually want to do *all* of the time in any situation. No one is horny *all* of the time. It just isn't humanly possible, even for guys. And although this isn't something they go around bragging about, it is nonetheless a fact of life.

It's one thing to know logically that guys aren't always horny, but it's quite another to understand that as it relates to your own sex and dating life. When you want to have sex and a guy doesn't, how do you feel? Confused? Insulted?

We can come up with a million creatively problematic reasons why a guy might not want to have sex. But the truth is, it's perfectly normal for a guy to not want to get laid in every situation possible. Maybe he's not in the mood, or maybe (if it's a guy you haven't slept with yet) he's actually thinking carefully about his choices.

If you've just started seeing a guy and he's not trying to have sex with you, don't freak out; maybe it's because he doesn't feel like he knows you well enough yet. One 25-year-old said, "For me, sex is an intimate experience. Once a connection is established it's enjoyable, but as someone who treats sex as a significant act, there are times when it's not appropriate."

"How soon is too soon?" is something guys think about as well. Just like us, guys are stuck in the damned-if-you-do, damned-if-you-don't cycle when it comes to sex. If he tries to initiate it too soon, you might think he's a jerk who "just wants one thing." Says a guy from San Francisco: "I definitely worry about coming across as a horny asshole if I'm with a girl I really like." Then on the other hand, if a guy doesn't try to have sex with you soon enough, he risks you worrying, "What's wrong with him?" Or even worse, putting him in "the friend zone." Complains a guy from Chicago: "I'm typically passive when it comes to sex, and never want to feel as if I'm pressuring someone into it. But my passivity can be exaggerated and 'the friend zone' is usually quicker to be tagged than anything else."

One day, you might even find yourself in a relationship with a guy who wants sex less than you do. And that still doesn't mean there is anything wrong with him. Says sex therapist Dr. Joy Davidson: "In any relationship where you have two unique people with different sexual histories and experiences, it's pretty unlikely that their sex drives would be perfectly in sync all of the time. Sometimes it's the guy's drive that's higher, and sometimes it's the girl's." If you're dating a guy whose sex drive is lower than yours, it's nothing to panic about, and in fact, it's much better for your relationship that you don't. One guy told me that his girlfriend wanting sex more often than he did caused a mild strain in the relationship, but because they "discussed it openly, it was less of an issue." Have the conversations you need to have in order to make sure that your sexual needs are being met, but know that his lower sex drive isn't a sign he's not into you.

There comes a time in every woman's life when she'll want to have sex and a guy won't. That's not because there's something wrong with him. It's not because he doesn't like you (assuming it's someone you're dating). It's not even because you don't make him horny, baby. It's because he's human, and sometimes, as one 28-year-old explained, he just "doesn't feel up to it."

When It Comes to Sex, Are Guys Thinking More Than Just "Score"?

Sam is the kind of good-looking guy who you'd just assume is a jerk. He's the head of security at a string of bars in New York, and is also an actor and athlete. His take on guys and sex, "Accept your dick size, deal with it, and move on." As cliché as it sounds, he thinks all guys' sexual issues are the result of insecurities about their penises.

That's right, guys' sexual issues. They have them. And they go deeper than just not being able to get laid. Even for guys, sex is complicated, although most aren't willing to talk about those complications as openly as they'll talk about wanting to get some. Though I had to dig for it, some guys were bold enough to open up to me about their concerns.

In keeping with Sam's theory, one guy confessed: "It doesn't matter what size you are, I think most guys fear that it won't be big enough." And another one told me: "I dated this girl who said her last boyfriend was huge. I was constantly worried that she was comparing me to him." Then he quickly reassured me (and himself): "I'm perfectly content with the size of my dick, but if this guy was 11 inches, how do you even compete with that? Seriously, I'm not small, I can tell you my measurements . . ." I politely declined the offer.

Guys worry about their equipment being adequate. They also worry about the presentation—there's a lot of manscaping going on these days. One guy told me: "Pretty much every guy I know at least trims to keep everything looking presentable." Although I've also heard guys groom themselves because it makes their dicks look bigger . . . which would bring us back to issue No. 1.

Even guys who are completely content with their size face a good deal of performance pressure when it comes to the physical act of sex. As a 23-year-old said, "Any guy who says he doesn't have insecurities about sex is lying. You want to be able to please the person you're sleeping with, and most guys worry about not being able to do that."

On a very basic level, in order for sex to happen, guys have to get hard and stay hard. I don't know if this is something we should be thankful for or not, but we can have sex even if our bodies aren't responding the way our minds are. For guys, that's just not the case. A 28-year-old told me: "Probably the biggest insecurity among me and my friends is what if you're with a girl and for some reason you don't get hard." Guys have to make sure they are "in the moment" enough to get hard, but then they also have to make sure they're not so "in the moment" they get off right away. As one New Yorker said: "No one wants to be a minute man." And although they don't want to be minute men, guys do feel pressure to get off eventually. A new study out of the University of Kansas shows that a full quarter of guys have faked an orgasm. Why? Because, just like us, they didn't want to hurt their partners' feelings by not getting off.

So here is a guy's sexual task: Get excited, wait . . . not too excited, come on buddy, get excited, finish up. We assume that guys have this really straightforward relationship with sex. Simply, "I'm horny, I want it." But it's not that simple. Guys have many concerns about sex, even if they don't parade around the locker room talking about them.

Is He Not Hard Because He's Not Attracted to Me?

One guy I interviewed told me: "It took me four tries to sleep with my girlfriend before I was able to get hard. I was too nervous. I physically can't have one-night stands; it's actually one of the things I like best about myself."

Erectile difficulties are something that happen to almost every guy at one point or another. So if you haven't encountered them yet, you likely will. Why are they so common? Because guys can feel a lot of pressure when it comes to sex, and that pressure isn't exactly arousing.

A 28-year-old in Denver told me: "The first time I have sex with a girl, there's a lot going through my head. I'm overly conscious of my performance because that will make or break you." And it's precisely that overconsciousness that causes guys to have trouble getting it up. According to a 22-year-old: "I've been in situations where I've psyched myself out, and it was with a girl I really liked, and she was into me too. It's one of those things that perpetuates itself because it doesn't happen, then you're wondering why it's not happening, and then you're out of the moment."

Ironically, it's the fear of not being able to get hard that's one of the most common reasons a guy doesn't. Either that, or alcohol, or general life stress. More rarely there may be some underlying medical cause. But the important thing to know is that it has *nothing* to do with you. In the words of one guy: "A lot of girls take it personally when a guy can't get it up. But it's really nothing to do with her. It could be how tired we are, or how much we've had to drink . . . but it's not because of her."

There are many reasons that a guy might go limp, but really, his penis problems are not your fault. If he tries to act like they are, it's just because he's embarrassed, insecure, and doesn't want to own up to what's going on. One guy divulged: "Times I can't get it up, I take it as such a blow to my manhood." Any guy who tells you you're the reason he can't perform is just trying to save face because he doesn't want to look like a dud. Look, if he was attracted enough to you to get in bed with you in the first place, he wants to have sex with you.

In general, men are not controlled by their penises. But this is one scenario where his penis does actually have a mind of its own. If you encounter a guy with erectile problems, the best thing you can do is reassure him it's not a big deal. When I asked guys what a girl in this situation should do, one answered: "Well, not getting angry or upset would be a start." Even if he's trying to act confident, a guy who's having trouble getting it up is probably feeling humiliated. And you don't want to get angry or upset with a guy over something that he can't control.

Another guy suggested: "The best thing a girl can do is get the guy out of his own head." Continue to make out with him to show you still think he's hot and still think he's "manly." Tell him not to worry about it, and that you're fine waiting for another night. Just take the focus away from his penis for a while . . . and who knows, something may just pop up.

Is He Not Going Down on Me Because He Thinks I'm Gross?

Your scent is powerful. Men are intoxicated by the aroma. You too should be empowered by your smell. Praise the earth mother my goddesses, *namaste*. Yeah, yeah, we've all been told how much guys supposedly like going down on girls. I've even preached it myself in lectures. But as easy of an idea as this is to regurgitate, it's a much harder one to actually believe.

Maybe because so few of us are actually comfortable with our vaginas ourselves? And if we don't love them, how can we expect a guy to? But getting to the bottom of this vagina thing: Do guys actually enjoy going down on girls? And when guys don't do it, is it because they think it's gross? Or is there some other reason?

Anecdotally, the resounding answer I got from many guys about going down on a girl was a unified "bring it." Guys like doing it, and they enjoy knowing they're doing something that pleases you. It is worth mentioning that a few guys I spoke with did have some funny takes on female anatomy. But their guy friends were always quick to put them in their place.

Guy: "I want this to go on the record! A girl going down on a guy, it's just skin. Guy going down on a girl, who knows what's going on down there!"

Friend (without missing a beat): "Dude! Sure, balls are just skin too, but they smell like shit! Vaginas are also *just* skin. Where the hell were you in anatomy class?"

Then in a separate incident with another group of guys:

Guy: "I like to go down on a girl when I know she's liking it. But the thing about vaginas is they have to be kept clean. It's like an asshole. It's a crevasse. You have to make sure to clean it well."

Friend (looking completely disgusted): "Wait, did you just compare a pussy to an asshole?"

Pussy, asshole, penis, whatever, I think we can all agree on the importance of hygiene. As a married 30-something said, "Sure, after we've been at an outdoor concert all day, that's not a time I would choose to go down on my wife. But assuming she's showered in the not-too-distant past, I love to do it."

On the follow-up survey I asked guys about their opinions of oral sex. I had a list of statements and told them to check all that apply. Here's what they said:

"How do you feel about going down on a girl?"

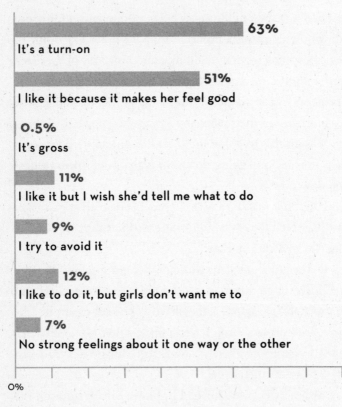

Almost two-thirds of guys are turned on by going down on you. But most important, very few guys think, "It's gross." (Only one out of the 200 that answered this survey.) And the few out there who do, would you really want to date them anyway? I mean, grow up, buddy. Or if you think vaginas are *so* gross, then start sleeping with dudes.

Some guys—though again pretty few—do try to avoid going down on a girl. But that could be because they're not sure what to do (the same way many girls feel about hand jobs, "What the hell am I doing here?").

Moral of the story: Don't be hesitant when a guy goes down on you. Enjoy it—he probably is. And if you end up in a relationship with a guy who doesn't do it that often, investigate why. It may be that he's just not sure what to do, or that he doesn't know you want him to try. But a guy who cares about you should care about your sexual pleasure. And for many girls that means that oral sex needs to be thrown into the mix. (If you don't want to have a verbal discussion about this, just drop a strong hint by anonymously sending your boyfriend a copy of Ian Kerner's *She Comes First*.)

Does He Want Feedback, or Should I Keep My Thoughts to Myself?

Just like we all "know" that guys like vaginas, we all "know" that, sexually speaking, guys want our feedback. Of course, that doesn't make it any easier to give. Even if we're not worried about offending a guy, it can feel awkward to start bossing him around. To us, giving instructions can feel like we're ruining the moment, but to them . . . it's actually hot.

According to the online survey, 58% of guys think it's "awesome" for girls they care about to give them instructions (in a nice way) for what to do in bed. They think it's awesome because "a girl knowing what she likes is hot." Another 25% of guys said they were "happy to get instructions for what to do better"—although they weren't cumming in their pants about it like the first group. 12% said they had mixed feelings because they wanted to know, "but it's awkward at the time." Only 1% of guys said they wanted to know "but it's also kind of offensive," and just 3% wanted you to "keep your feelings to yourself." Now, if this is not a clear indication to speak your mind in the bedroom, I don't know what is. All you have to decide is how to bring it up.

One guy suggested you "take control, grab my hand and say, 'No, dude, this way.'" Personally, I think use of the word "dude" in the middle of a sex act may be a bit of a turnoff. But showing a guy, instead of telling him, is certainly a decent option. That way it's *very* clear what you want.

If you're going to give a guy verbal feedback, be sure to frame it in a positive light. Many guys agreed that how they got instructions mattered. As much as guys do want direction, they don't want their sexual egos obliterated. One from Houston said, "It depends how she says it. If she goes, 'You suck at this,' that's not cool. Instead she should say something like, 'Next time do this.' Or bring it up as it's happening. If she says, 'I like it like this,' or 'Do it this way,' it's hot; it doesn't ruin the moment. The key is confidence, 'Here is how I want it done.'"

Show your confidence, and tell a guy what you like. Though you may feel awkward about it, your guy probably doesn't. Either way, a little awkwardness today in exchange for better sex tomorrow seems like a pretty fair trade to me.

Are Guys Destined to Cheat?

I met Marilynn on a train when she put me out of my computer frustration by telling me that Amtrak Wi-Fi never works on Macs. She's a vivacious 50-something, and I quickly became obsessed with her. Every now and then, you meet someone who's just breathtaking—some combination of physical looks and overall demeanor that makes them magnetic in a way that transcends age. *Exquisite*, as that word might be applied to a person, is the only way I can think to describe her.

Our conversation quickly progressed from computers to personal lives . . . as is often the case when you meet women on trains. You probably think I'm going to tell you she was cheated on. I'm not. Instead, she talked to me about being madly in love with her boyfriend of three years. The only problem with the relationship . . . he's married.

Yes, I was sitting across from—and engaged in a conversation with—the other woman. And the worst part was, I was sort of on her side. According to her, her boyfriend's marriage was miserable. He and his wife basically hate each other, but his wife won't get a divorce because she's addicted to their lifestyle (he makes lots of money, they live in a big house, belong to a fancy country club, etc.). He won't get a divorce because he's terrified his kids will hate him if he leaves.

I would never endorse cheating. But I do think it's important to think about some of the cheating statistics we hear within context. When cheating happens, it's not always like Jesse James, Tiger Woods, or Arnold Schwarzenegger . . . affairs seemingly out of the blue in perfectly happy and healthy relationships. When cheating happens, it's often in dissatisfied relationships that may end in a breakup or divorce.

How common is cheating? Well, we don't really know. It's a hard thing to measure because, obviously, people who've done it tend to keep it private. But according to one widely cited study, about 50% to 60% of men and 45% to 55% of women cheat at some point during their marriages.[3] Cheating is clearly a very real problem. But it's a problem for both men and women. Is he destined to cheat? Only about as destined as you are.

I asked guys: "Would you cheat on your girlfriend if you knew you wouldn't get caught?" Twenty-one percent of guys said yes. I happened to catch one guy in the process of answering the question, and got to hear his thought process:

Him: "I'm really struggling with question 31. I don't know what to say."

Me: "Well, it's pretty straightforward; either you'd cheat or you wouldn't."

Him: "It depends on who, though. If I was dating 'the one,' was in love with her, and thought I could marry her, no, I wouldn't cheat. But if I was dating a girl I wasn't in love with and then had the opportunity to be with a girl I've had a crush on my whole life, then yeah, I'd probably cheat. So, I guess that means I have to check 'yes.'"

This conversation made me wonder: How many of the guys I surveyed would cheat in a more casual relationship, but not a serious one? If we're willing to look at cheating on a scale from immoral to insanely screwed up, the situation matters.

So on the follow-up survey I framed it this way: "Would you

cheat on a girl you were in love with and thought might be the one?" In that situation, only 14% of guys said yes. Being in love with someone didn't eliminate the possibility of cheating, but it did at least reduce it.

Another important question is: What do guys consider to be cheating? Is cuddling cheating? Is kissing cheating? Or in order for it to be cheating does it have to involve a genital (or even two)?

"If you had engaged in the following activities with a girl who isn't your girlfriend, would you consider it cheating?"

44% yes
Emotional affair (excessive e-mailing, phone calls, texts, etc.)

69% yes
Cuddling

81% yes
Kissing

95% yes
Oral sex

98% yes
Intercourse

0%   100%

I'm not sure who these guys are who don't consider sex cheating. They must have either misread the question, or just don't believe in monogamy. But here's where it gets interesting: Guys in a serious relationship were only somewhat less likely to say they'd cheat than guys overall (17% versus 22%). *But* their definition of cheating got much stricter. This is how guys in a serious relationship compare to the rest:

"If you had engaged in the following activities with a girl who isn't your girlfriend, would you consider it cheating?"

52% yes
43% yes
Emotional affair

83% yes
67% yes
Cuddling

88% yes
80% yes
Kissing

99% yes
95% yes
Oral sex

100% yes
98% yes
Intercourse

0%   100%

SERIOUS RELATIONSHIP
NOT A SERIOUS RELATIONSHIP

Either guys get more virtuous after they've fallen in love, or more virtuous guys get into serious relationships. Either way, once you're serious with a guy, he'll likely have stricter standards when it comes to cheating. Hooray for boyfriends.

The most important part of the cheating puzzle, though, is the "why." Is men's cheating really as simple as "he can't keep his dick in his pants"? Because that's usually how it's explained: "Of course a guy is going to cheat! It's inevitable; he can't control himself. If there's a hot girl who wants him, it's just too big of a temptation."

But like many of the things we're told about men's sexuality, this is another one that's just not true. M. Gary Neuman is a family counselor and the author of *The Truth About Cheating*. For his book, he interviewed men about why they cheated and found that "for 92% of men living in the United States, cheating is not primarily about sex." He also found that only 12% of men who cheated said their mistresses were more physically attractive than their wives. The real reason men cheat? Emotional dissatisfaction. They feel underappreciated and emotionally disconnected. That's right, back to the chapter about guys and relationships—guys have feelings too. The way to a man's heart may be through his stomach, but the way to a man's penis is through his heart.

Houston: We Have a Problem

"Have you ever eaten pussy?!?!"

I was in the middle of a pretty deep conversation about relationships with four guys at an outdoor pub in Rice Village when things started deteriorating rapidly. In economics, they call this phenomenon diminishing rate of return, the point at which the amount of effort you put in stops being reflected in the amount of product being put out. This is what happens when talking to guys about sex. It takes a while for them to take it seriously, they get increasingly thoughtful for an hour or two, then after too long, things start going south. In this instance things had gone south quite literally as one guy kept shouting across the table at another, "Dude, have you ever gone down on a girl?"

The anti-cunnilinger in question, a 29-year-old I should add, stayed mum. "You're not the journalist here. I'm not talking to you about it."

They all looked at me. "Fine." I took the bait: "Have you ever eaten pussy?"

He hesitated for a second. "No, I have not."

This blew my mind. He was 29. Had been in relationships—one that lasted for six months! Had had sex. Had never gone down on a girl? How does that sort of thing happen? "What do you mean, you've never gone down on a girl? How is that possible?"

"I don't know," he defended himself. "I guess it's never come up."

"What do you mean, 'never come up'?!?"

"A girl has never asked me to do it. And it's fourth—or maybe fifth—on my list of what I would do."

"What's your list?" I was shocked.

"Hmmm. If it were up to me . . . the pecking order of how I would do things . . . first sex, like, vaginal sex. Second, I'd have a girl go down on me. Third, anal . . ."

"Anal?!? What girl is going to let you have anal sex with her if you've never gone down on her?"

He ignored the question and kept going: "Fourth . . . ummm, man . . . I don't know how to say this. I'm a gentleman . . ." He hesitated and for the first time during this entire conversation started to look uncomfortable. "All right, I'm just going to say it . . . TITTY FUCKING!" he screamed.

The entire table erupted with laughter, but he went on: "Is there a better way to put it? That's more polite? A scientific term or something? Like, 'breast penetration'?"

He wasn't being facetious with this question, either. He was genuinely worried about being offensive with the phrase *titty fucking* and ironically unfazed by the fact that oral sex on a girl was last on his sexual to-do list. The funniest thing about this kid is that he was a decent guy. He had spent the past hour talking about different girls he had dated and was by no means a selfish jerk. It's not that he didn't care about women's sexual pleasure; I just don't think he understood it.

SEEMINGLY ASSHOLE MINDSETS WE SHOULD ADOPT FOR OURSELVES

Thinking about some of guys' asshole behaviors (or seemingly asshole behaviors), it occurred to me . . . some of these mindsets are ones we should adopt for ourselves! It's good to look out for yourself when it comes to relationships—not so much so that you hurt other people or completely neglect their needs—but enough that you ensure your own needs are being met. A certain amount of selfishness is necessary when dating because looking out for yourself is *your* responsibility and no one else's. The following are some "asshole" commandments that many girls could stand to embrace.

Don't Be Afraid of Rejection

There's a reason that seemingly douchey guys with cheesy lines still do well with girls. Sheer numbers. If a guy hits on every girl in the bar, chances are he'll stumble upon one who will go out with him. But to get to that one, he can't let the rejection of the first 20 get to him.

The best way to meet guys is to start talking to them—anywhere and everywhere. But to do this, you have to get over whatever part of you thinks you can't, it's scary, or you're "not that outgoing." You also have to get over the fear that you might show interest in a guy who doesn't show any back. As the pickup books for guys preach, "If you want to pick up a girl, you can't be afraid of being rejected by her." The same goes for picking up guys. Because if you're scared about the possibility of rejection, you're never going to have the guts to approach guys in the first place.

Here's how to get over your fear of rejection: Take a second right now to think about the worst-case scenario. Seriously, what's the absolute worst that can happen? You start talking to a guy, he doesn't seem that interested, then he walks away. Or you Facebook message a crush to see if he wants to get together sometime and he never responds. Then what? Well, nothing.

First of all, it's not like you confessed: "I have a giant crush on you and want a life-size picture of your face hanging over my bed." All you're saying by reaching out or approaching a guy is "you seem kinda cool." And is that really so embarrassing of a confession?

Be okay with rejection, but also know that as a girl, you're going to get rejected a lot less—because most guys are impressed when a girl takes the initiative. And if you do get rejected, since a girl hitting on a guy isn't perceived as threatening or skeevy, you're going to get turned down in a much nicer way than you might shoot down a guy. As a 31-year-old from Seattle complained: "Girls act like bitches to dudes, like every dude who's interested is a potential rapist."

Perhaps you're not that harsh, but think of the ways that girls can sidestep a guy's advances. It's usually something to the tune of "Eww, get away from me." A guy is never going to be that rude to a girl; the worst he's going to do is act uninterested or just be unresponsive. Wait . . . I take that back. I was in a club in Miami once when a guy actually gave my friend a "talk to the hand." But on the off chance something like that happens to you, the story is so good it's worth it.

Sure, no one wants to get rejected. But the truth is, it stings for a second, and then you move on. Just like wearing a thong, plucking your eyebrows, or waxing your bikini line, the first few times may be startling, but then you just get used to it.

Practice makes perfect—that's another thing those pickup books preach. Start talking to guys. If it doesn't go well or you feel awkward, get back up on the horse and try again. Really, what do you have to lose?

Assholes may get the girls, but that's only because they're the ones who put themselves out there. If you aren't willing to make the first move, then you're stuck with whatever guy decides *he* wants to put the moves on you. That means eliminating the shyer, less flashy, and (probably) less sketchy guys from your dating pool. Even worse, it means passing up opportunities to have meaningful relationships with great guys. It's always better to risk rejection than risk losing what could be the love of your life. And even if you do get rejected, wouldn't you rather know that at least you tried?

Be the One in Control

If guys hold the power in dating situations, it is only because we've given it to them. We give them control by following stereotypical dating roles that make them the deciders (because "guys are the ones who are supposed to initiate everything"). *They* get to decide to ask for our number, *they* get to decide if they want to ask us out, and after a date *they* get to decide if they want to call again. We're in the vulnerable position because we're the ones left waiting. And only if a guy likes us enough can the relationship progress.

Because customary dating traditions are set up to be so entirely reliant on a guy's actions, it can obscure the reality that relationships are about *two* people deciding if they like each other—not a guy deciding if *he* wants to move forward. But since we're so focused on what *he's* doing and what *he* thinks, it takes the attention away from what *we* think. It's all, "Is *he* going to call," instead of, "Do *we* want to hear from him?"

Think about if the situation were reversed. If you were the one responsible for pushing the relationship forward, you'd really have to evaluate your feelings. Do you like this guy enough to go through the effort of figuring out what to say on a phone call? (Because as the person initiating the call, the onus is kind of on you to keep the conversation flowing.) Do you like him enough to deal with complications of planning a date? (And probably dropping a good amount of cash to go on it?) Did the date go well enough that you want to spend even more money taking him out again? (Because he might still expect you to pay.) When all you have to do is pick up a call or show up on a date, it just doesn't force you to be picky in the same way.

Screw dating traditions. You should spend more time in the driver's seat—because that's the way to have more control over your love life. When you meet a guy, get his number instead of (or at least in addition to) giving him yours. He can sweat it out and constantly check the volume of his ringer, while you hem and haw over whether or not he's worth your time and energy. After a first date, be the one to say, "I'll call you." Or if he says it first, respond, "I'll think about picking up." There's no reason you can't be the one calling the shots and taking the initiative.

At the very least, you can vow to analyze your feelings independent of a guy's actions. The day after meeting him (and likely a day or two before he calls), decide what you thought. Did he actually seem cool or was that the beer goggles? After a date assess: Did he talk about himself too much? Did he have a bad attitude or bad personality? Did he seem a little bit entitled or rude? And at that point, make a decision about whether or not the relationship should move forward. Don't let some guy who kinda sucked trick you into seeing him again because you're so preoccupied with his feelings that you're ignoring your own.

Don't Automatically Assume
You Want a Relationship

The message that "men don't want relationships" is one that no doubt confuses and debilitates many guys. But by that same token, hearing that all you want as a woman *is* a relationship has in some ways debilitated us. It can make us mistakenly assume we should want to commit to any guy who puts forth the effort to take us to dinner. It can also make us try so hard to make a relationship work that we overlook the fact we're getting involved with the wrong guy.

Due to the misconception that men are perpetually avoiding relationships while women are perpetually searching for them, our relationship priorities have gotten a bit mixed up. For many of us (consciously or not), our first goal after meeting a guy is to try to get him to be our boyfriend. Then, oddly, the second is to decide how much we like him. We've learned to approach dating this way because what's the point of deciding you really like a guy if he's inevitably not going to commit to you—it's a self-preservation thing, really. But now that we know guys actually want relationships, it's time for a priority shift.

First, when you meet a guy, don't automatically assume your goal should be to start a relationship with him. He doesn't get to jump right into the "I want you to be my boyfriend" slot. He should have to earn his place there. It's okay to want a relationship in general, but you should only want a relationship with a specific guy after he's proved himself to be "boyfriend material." (You know, smart, thoughtful, funny, treats you well, and has a personality that's compatible with yours.) You may know that a guy is someone you're interested in dating right away. But withhold judgment about whether or not you want to be exclusive until you get to know him better, and figure out how well the two of you connect.

Second, just because a guy may be willing to commit to you doesn't necessarily mean you should commit to him. Guys, on the whole, want relationships. Finding one who will be your boyfriend isn't the equivalent of unearthing a buried treasure. It's great that he's into you, but pay attention to your feelings too. Consider the fact that your interest in him could be primarily physical. Or that while you're enjoying his company, ultimately he's not the one for you. And even if he's theoretically "perfect," notice if there's something about him or the relationship that just feels off.

Third, your goal should not be to "have a relationship"; it should be to "find a good relationship." Our whole lives we've been told not to give up—that if things aren't working out, we should just try harder. But early dating relationships are one place where you should do just the opposite. If things don't feel right two or three months into dating someone, don't try harder to make it work; take the hint that it's not supposed to. In the beginning, a relationship should just be easy. As everyone says, when you meet the right person, it will just click. If you have to talk yourself into liking a guy, explain away incompatibilities, or just don't totally get along with him . . . it's time to give up.

A 30-year-old guy from New York told me: "I've had a few relationships where I felt like the girl and I both knew that we weren't really falling for each other, but she wanted to make it work regardless. Once we were in dating mode, she seemed more committed to having a relationship than figuring out if we were right for each other."

In a similar vein, I know a girl who will spend hours complaining about her boyfriend, about things he does that she doesn't like, and how she's just not sure it's the right match. Then in the next breath she'll be talking about wanting to get engaged to him. It makes me want to slap her: "Are you crazy? How are you thinking about getting engaged to a guy you're so unsure about?" I get that she's ready to be in a committed relationship, but she's so wrapped up in the idea of a commitment that she's not being picky enough about who she's committing to.

It's human to want to be in a relationship, fall in love, and ultimately find someone to spend your life with. But never let the urge to take those steps overshadow the reality of who you're taking those steps with.

Feel Entitled When It Comes to Sex

Recently a 28-year-old girl said to me: "You know, if I had to give up one thing in my relationship, it would be sex. I guess I've just never been that much of a sex person. Like, if I had some weird condition and doctors told me I could never do it again, I'd be okay with it."

Twenty-eight and ready to give up on sex—when you hear something like that, do you laugh or cry? The worst part is that I'm sure she's not alone in thinking this way.

The average age for a girl to start having sex is 18, but many women don't start having orgasms until sometime in their 20s. And our "sexual peak"—we're not supposed to reach that until sometime in our 30s. So we're talking about a handful of years of bad sex, followed by a decade or so of mediocre sex, but then don't worry, about 15-plus years after losing your V-card you might actually start having regular orgasms.

I'd like to let you in on a little secret. You know why we're not hitting our sexual peak earlier? At least in part because we're worrying too much about our guys and not enough about ourselves. Younger women tend to focus more on the emotional aspects of sex and a guy's sexual pleasure. It's not until we're older that we start paying more attention to our own physical enjoyment and what makes us feel good.[1] Meanwhile, guys are working in reverse. Many younger guys focus their sexual attention exclusively on themselves. Then as they get older, they start to realize, "Golly gee, there's someone else in this equation who should be enjoying themselves too!"[2] Now is it really any wonder that we're not having more regular orgasms when our first sexual years are so completely cock-centric?

Many women don't get off regularly. This is an important thing to consider when thinking about sex drive. Can you imagine being able to walk into a sexual encounter with almost 100% certainty you're going to get off? No wonder guys want to have sex so much! Maybe guys want to have sex more often, but that's not because they're innately hornier than we are; it's because they have a better risk/reward ratio. When a girl has sex she might become pregnant, because of her anatomy she is twice as likely to get an STD, there's the whole "slut" thing, and then even after risking all that, she probably won't even get off! So yeah, maybe a girl is more hesitant to have sex at the beginning of a relationship, or wants sex less often within a relationship, but it's not because she's not horny.

Women have strong sex drives, and those sex drives matter. We have to recognize this because if we don't, we get caught in a self-perpetuating downward spiral: We don't get off much, so we don't want to have sex much. We don't want to have sex much, so presumably our sex drives must not be that strong (or important to us). Our sex drives aren't that strong, so it's not that important we have an orgasm . . . and this mentality is *why* we don't get off much.

If you had sex with a guy and he didn't have an orgasm, you would probably feel pretty bad, right? You'd likely be thinking, "We'd better do this again in the morning so that poor thing doesn't leave with blue balls." Why do we think this way? Because guys are really horny, so they *really* have to get off. Well, guess what? You're horny too, and you're just as entitled to an orgasm as a guy. A guy should feel just as obligated to satisfy you as you feel to satisfy him. Yes, it may be more difficult for you to get off, but that doesn't mean he gets to slack off and not even try.

If you're like most girls, you could probably stand to be more selfish in the bedroom. Forget the thoughts of "How do I look?" or "What's he thinking right now?" or "Am I giving him enough positive feedback?" You're on his penis; he's fine. Think about yourself. Think about what positions feel good for you. Think about how to tactfully communicate that you want him to last long enough for you to get yours (on average 20 minutes), or how to make clear when he needs to call in some backups (be it his tongue or his fingers). Feel entitled to having an orgasm, and make figuring out your sexual enjoyment a priority—on your own if need be (yes, I'm telling you to masturbate), and when you're with a guy.

Look at the Opposite Sex as Hormonal

Stereotypically, guys see girls as emotionally high maintenance. When pursuing a relationship, they know they have to look out for our feelings, listen to us after we've had a bad day, and do nice things to make us feel appreciated. Well, it turns out, these requirements swing both ways. Guys may not get periods, but they still have to be treated with the same type of sensitivity they assume is required by us.

According to relationship expert M. Gary Neuman in *The Truth About Cheating*: "Men need to hear how wonderful they are and be appreciated for what they do right. The big lie we keep hearing over and over again is that women are the emotional ones, whereas men are like rocks, doing their thing, needing only lots of sex to be happy." That's right, we have to appeal to men's emotional needs as much as we appeal to their physical ones.

This concept was supported again by a family friend I ran into recently who got divorced a few years ago. Like most people after hearing the topic of my book, he was eager to share his theories.

"It's like this, whether you're the A guy who kills the animal, the B guy who throws it on the truck, or the C guy who cleans up afterward, every guy needs to feel like what he does is important. He needs the woman in his life to act like he has the hardest, most valuable job in the world. That's how you keep a man happy in a relationship."

I don't think it's quite that simple, but I do think his basic message is spot-on. Guys—and, really, all people—need to feel that the person they're dating respects them and thinks they're important.

In the bigger sense, what my family friend and M. Gary Neuman are getting at is that you have to look out for a guy's emotional needs. That's not relationship advice you get very often. And as a result, on some level we might assume, "Oh, he's a guy, he doesn't sweat the small stuff." But that's just not true.

Guys get their feelings hurt too. Assume that if you blow off plans, don't pay attention to him, or don't show him enough affection, it's going to upset him. Assume that when you're mean to him, it hurts his feelings and, in turn, the relationship. If you've just had a big fight or confrontation, expect that he might be a little standoffish until he fully recovers from the trauma. The golden rule is key here: Treat others (even guys) how you want to be treated. If you're acting in a way that would upset you, it will likely upset him.

Even in a Relationship, Be Self-Centered

Throughout my research, I wavered constantly between man loving and man hating. Occasionally, when I talked to a guy for long enough, my feelings about him would swing just as wildly. One night I had been talking to a group of guys, and the one directly across the table from me was the loudest and most obnoxious. "It's like this," he kept explaining. "I started out as a sperm. Then ever since I was 12, I've been a raging hard-on." Every now and then throughout the conversation he would piggyback on someone else's comment: "because guys are giant erections." But when the conversation turned to relationships, he abandoned his boner remarks for ones that were more thoughtful:

"If you're going to be in a serious relationship, you have to know what you want first. Otherwise you shoot in the dark and have unsuccessful relationship after unsuccessful relationship. Before you can be serious with someone, you have to figure out: What do you want out of life? How are you going to get there? What kind of father do you want to be? Do you want to be in the rat race? Or do you want to be able to homeschool your kids? Before you can figure out your relationship, you have to figure out yourself."

His friends were as shocked as I was over his sudden transformation. One turned to him, taken aback: "Whoa, dude, that was some really philosophical shit."

"Yeah," he answered urgently. "She's trying to write a book here!" (I guess that fact hadn't completely sunk in during our first hour of conversation.)

Like boner-man said, before you can expect to be in a good relationship, you have to spend time figuring out yourself, and what you want out of life. It's important for any relationship to have mutual goals, but you need your own goals too. If you don't have them, your boyfriend's goals become your goals, and your life gets completely consumed by his. And then, you end up completely dependent—not a situation that's comfortable for anyone involved. If you want to have a healthy and balanced relationship, you can't center your life around your boyfriend; you have to center it around yourself.

My 25-year-old (male) cousin said to me recently, "For the first time in seven years I have to decide what to do with my life, because I'm not basing it on what my girlfriend needs." My cousin is funny. He dates girls who are superambitious, going-to-save-the-world doctor types, but smart as he is, he's had the same dead-end job since graduating from college. Not surprisingly, his girlfriends outgrow him then move on. From an outside perspective, his relationship problems are clear: No girl is going to commit to him until he develops his own plan and his own goals. And that self-sufficiency is something that both *guys* and *girls* look for in a mate. In relationships, people want someone who's going to grow beside them, not wrapped around them, hanging on for dear life.

If you want to date an amazing guy, you have to be an amazing girl: Have your own interests, hobbies, and passions; be your own person. Spend more time focusing on who you are than what you look like. I'm not saying this to be cheesy and make you feel good; I'm saying it because I know the type of girls who great guys end up with—the ones who are confident, have a strong sense of themselves, and have their own priorities. In the words of a 28-year-old from Denver: "Women should look within to find out who they are and what is important. No guy can fulfill your life, but being true to yourself can attract a guy worth sharing the experiences of life with."

Equally as important as developing your own priorities is keeping focus on those priorities once you're in a relationship. It's true, all relationships will require some amount of compromise, but never give up your dreams, your interests, or your independent life. To some extent you have to remain focused on yourself, because having your own life is what's going to keep you happy and fulfilled. And you know what—it's also what's going to keep your relationship interesting years down the road. If you and your boyfriend essentially become the same being, then of course the relationship will get boring . . . there's only one person in it.

Keeping yourself a priority also means keeping your friends. It's great to hang out with your boyfriend's friends, but only up to a point. Never forget that when it comes down to it, they are *his* friends. And if you break up, they will revert back to him. Even if you don't break up, having other friends is going to keep a healthy amount of space and balance in your relationship.

If you don't have your own friends, then when "guys' night" rolls around you're going to be left home alone feeling abandoned and jealous. No one needs that. What you need is to be out with a crew of your own. And I wish I didn't have to explicitly say this, but one that is fun, supportive, and makes you feel good. What I'm hinting at here is, if your current group of friends are backstabbing bitches, find better ones—ones you *actually* enjoy. Not only do you need friends, but you need friends you're genuinely psyched to hang out with—people you like enough that you'll want to make time for, even if you're head over heels in love with some guy.

If you have friends you like and passions that excite you, keeping a life that's separate from your boyfriend happens naturally, and by default, keeping a healthy balance does too. Even 20 years from now, if you're married with kids, that balance is what's going to help keep the spark alive. So while there are many sacrifices you will make for the sake of a relationship, giving up your own life should never be one of them. You should always remain, at least partially, self-centered.

At first glance, these asshole commandments may seem a bit, well, assholey. But being selfish—in a controlled way—is a good thing for relationships. Guys complain about having girlfriends who are "naggy" and "always getting upset," and that's what happens when you completely neglect your needs and only look out for someone else's. You can do that for a while, but in time you'll get fed up and become completely resentful toward your boyfriend because of all the sacrifices you've made on his behalf.

Don't let that happen. Instead, stay a little self-centered from the very beginning. When you're getting involved with a guy, make sure he's really a guy you want, not one you're settling for and are going to get annoyed with as soon as things get comfortable. As the relationship progresses, don't lose sight of your goals or let his priorities overshadow yours. Make sure he's doing what it takes to please you sexually, so that sex is something you want to do for your own pleasure, and not just his. By continuing to prioritize your needs, you can best ensure happiness for both you and your boyfriend throughout your relationship.

New York: Welcome, Bitch

I met "Sniffles" on Bedford Avenue in Williamsburg, Brooklyn. We talked for at least an hour, and I have pages of notes from our conversation, but somehow I neglected to write down his name. What I can tell you about him is that he was tall, 29, had a beard, and had a cold. He had just run out to get a coffee, and I'm sure hadn't anticipated talking to someone on the street for an hour. As a result, he had no tissues on him, so as we talked he had to continually wipe his nose on the sleeve of his hoodie.

"Dating in New York is like the Cuban Missile Crisis. Every one here is so hard and jaded. When you first move, you're not like that. Then you get royally fucked by someone and you pay it forward to someone else. It's like, 'Welcome to New York, bitch!'"

The pay-it-forward phenomenon may happen to an extreme in New York, but people do it everywhere. We've all been screwed over at some point in our lives; then, instead of focusing our anger on the one person who screwed us, we develop a general hatred for the entire opposite sex. We cultivate a mistrust and give ourselves an imaginary pass to treat them however we want to—because, Mommy! They hit us first!

When we look at all the crappy ways guys treat girls, we wonder: Are they driven to do these things because of their biology? Or maybe it's our culture? But what if instead it's their defense from past painful experiences? Maybe they got really hurt by some girl, and now they're convinced (as I heard many say) that "women are evil." The 35% of guys who would lie about their relationship intentions in order to sleep with a girl, I wonder how many of them have been totally burned by a girl they liked, or even loved. And I wonder, how many of them think that they're allowed to treat girls like shit because they were once treated like shit by a girl.

Guys are not alone in this war against the opposite sex. Judging even by the title of this book, we're just as guilty. When a guy takes you on a date and you're not feeling it, it doesn't seem so unreasonable to just ignore his calls. And it feels completely justified because we think, "Why should I have to be nice to him? He's a guy." They've been inconsiderate to us, so it feels like we should get to be inconsiderate right back.

But here's the thing: There is no "they." It's not like all men are one giant mass, and treating one of them badly will end up getting back at that complete jackass who hurt you in college. And because there is no "they," you cannot hold one guy's actions against another one. It's no use being generally pissed at men because men didn't treat you badly—*a* man did.

It's normal to have baggage. But every guy who comes into your life deserves a clean slate. It's unproductive to assume that just because one guy acted a certain way, another guy is bound to do the same thing. And it's not fair to make an innocent man pay for the way a guilty one treated you.

"Everyone has a natural defense mechanism and is afraid of being too 'soft,'" says Sniffles. "But what's your alternative, be hard and jaded and never let anyone know who you really are?"

Don't let a few experiences with assholes keep you from being able to open up to a good guy when he comes along. If you let some past jerk keep you from future happiness, then you let the assholes win. But by moving on and being willing to open yourself up again—*that* is your best revenge.

CASE STUDY: ERIK

Erik is a 27-year-old lawyer I met in Seattle. He's tall, blond, and handsome enough, though perhaps a bit into himself. There was a sense of entitlement about him that was confirmed after he forwarded me an e-mail from a girl who had ended things after a few dates. "Mature of her to go through the trouble of explaining how and why things went wrong," I wrote him. He wrote back: "Wait, you think doing this through e-mail is mature?"

Yeah, I do. And I stand by that answer. After three dates, you're lucky to get an "I don't see this going anywhere" instead of just a blank cell-phone screen. A full e-mail explaining *why* it's not going anywhere is above and beyond the call of duty. Dater of the Year!

The most interesting thing about Erik's breakup, though (if we can even call it that), is that he was convinced it was his fault. "I was giving her the full-court press, telling her I liked her a lot. I was being too available." He gave me an elaborate schedule of their texting interactions and told me how he took a day off because her texts back the day before were short. But the straw that he thinks broke the camel's back was the fact that after their third date, when they were making out, he put his hand up her shirt.

Listening to him recount every detail of this affair sounded ridiculous. I wanted to scream at him, "It's nothing you did, bozo! She just doesn't like you." But as idiotic as he looked from where I was standing, I know that we've all been there.

The problem is, when it's you, you're blind. Like a sports fan who's convinced it's *his* lucky underwear that caused his team to win, we mistakenly think that these small things we do when dating are the make-it-or-break-it factors.

But here is the truth: If someone likes you, they like you. If they don't, they don't. For all the elaborate reasons we can come up with about why, the truth is they just weren't feeling it. It's easier to stomach that it had to do with the amount we called, that we texted back too fast, or that we looked too available. It's harder to face the fact that it's just us.

But in the same way that it can make us feel powerless—knowing there's no magic pattern of ignoring that will manipulate someone into falling for you—it's also kind of liberating. There is nothing we can do. Which means there's no reason to stress about the small stuff, because it just doesn't matter. If you want to call a guy, call him. If you want to ask him to do something, do it. The writing is already on the wall, and an extra text or invite isn't going to change that.

There is, however, an asterisk on all of this. It doesn't matter what we do as long as we (a) act within the range of normal and (b) conduct ourselves in a way that commands respect.

What do I mean by "normal"? When you're getting to know someone, you're on the lookout for anybody who's a psycho killer, insanely high maintenance, incredibly sketchy, or just a wet blanket. It doesn't matter if you text a guy back right away. It *does* matter if you text him repeatedly after no response, at really inappropriate times, or say things that make you look sketchy: "I kow this is the 345th text I send you today LOL! Its 3am Im so hammered, can't fond my walet and leavin wit some guy named Billy he sad hed walk me home." Basically, don't text him any amount or message that would indicate, "This chick is a train wreck."

What do I mean by "respect"? Don't drop everything at his beck and call. If a guy gets in touch with you drunk from a bar, don't ditch your friends and come running. If he tries to make you his booty call, don't let him (unless, of course, that's all you want from him). And if he wants to hang out at a time that is inconvenient for you, make a counteroffer for a day that works better. Showing respect for yourself means making it clear you have your own life, your own priorities, and you're not going to let someone treat you in a way that you don't want to be treated.

HOW TO IDENTIFY ONE, BREAK FREE, OR GET ONE TO CHANGE HIS TUNE

The True Prevalence of Assholes

"You want to know about guys? I'll tell you about guys. I'm a blue-collar worker, so I'm a real man, unlike these Ivy League types around here." A construction worker from Florida stopped me at a bar in Atlanta when he found out what I was doing. "It's like this. You grow up puttin' on this act that you're tough, only want sex, and things don't affect you. You think the only way girls'll like you is if you act like that. If they knew who you really were, they wouldn't. All your friends act the same way, so you can't let them know who you are either. Then one day, you fall in love, and you realize you don't have to pretend to be somethin' you're not. You open up to a girl and know that she'll love you for who you are . . . and then, you go out and get yourself some new friends."

It seems crazy, but many guys say they act (or *acted*) like assholes for our sake. The shared sentiment among many I spoke with was this: "I'll stop being an asshole when girls stop going for assholes." From a 35-year-old I met at a farmer's market in LA: "Women are so strange, in my experience with them. I could treat the same girl with kindness and respect and she would turn away. I could reverse it so quickly by being a jerk and she would turn back. That's in relationships and meeting them for the first time." From a 24-year-old I met at a bar in Atlanta: "Guys act like jerks because if you are too nice you will not be taken seriously." And from a 26-year-old I met on North Beach in Chicago: "Guys are usually selfish and jerks to girls. BUT girls seem to respond positively to those guys most of the time." And as a different guy observed: "What gets rewarded gets repeated."

Many guys will act macho, sex hungry, and emotionally uninvested because they think that's the type of alpha male that, deep down, women are attracted to. Why don't guys show they're actually nicer and more sensitive? They're afraid to because they think we won't like it. That's right—like exotic birds, the asshole dance is something many guys do to attract us.

Of course for some guys, being an asshole isn't a put-on mating call: It's actually their true colors. All guys aren't assholes. Most guys aren't assholes. But 16% of them probably are.

To come up with this number, I went back over my data and assigned positive asshole points for questions guys answered like a dick, and negative asshole points for questions they answered like a great guy. Depending on how many points they scored, I placed guys in one of five categories: true assholes, misguided, human, good guys, and saints. A list of the questions and scoring system I used is given in Appendix 3, "Quantifying an Asshole." Here's how guys netted out on the asshole continuum:

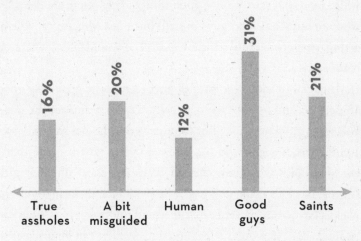

Using my scale, 16% of guys are true assholes. This means they don't care much about your feelings, they're likely to be cheaters, they will act sexually irresponsible with little remorse, and they'd probably be crappy boyfriends. On top of that 16%, there's another 20% who aren't real assholes but are a little misguided. Maybe they haven't quite figured out they have feelings, and still think that sleeping with as many girls as possible is the key to their happiness. For the most part, these guys are probably young and immature, and will hopefully grow out of it. They're the kind of guys who may be inconsiderate hookups but, if they fall for you, pretty decent boyfriends.

On the other end of the spectrum, about 21% of guys out there are true saints. Completely dedicated boyfriends, overly considerate hookups, and guys you don't have to worry about in any situation. Basically, real softies who, other guys might say, end up in "the friend zone." On top of that is another 31% who are great guys, generally trustworthy, but don't live and die by your every whim (and that's probably a good thing). Then there are the 12% who are human. Good guys overall, but ones who are capable of acting irresponsible and selfish. Especially, I would guess, where sex is concerned.

The final breakdown: 84% of guys seem to be genuinely good at the core, and 64% of them actually act like it most of the time. Yes, some guys are scum. But for every guy who has screwed over a girl, there is a girl who has screwed over a guy. It's true that I talked to guys who have cheated or would cheat on their girlfriends. But I also talked to guys who would never dream of cheating but have been cheated on, sometimes multiple times. Men can be insensitive to women's feelings, and women can be insensitive right back. As one guy complained on his survey: "Men are treated like commodities by women, used and discarded. If you don't have what's on their list of things they want, you're gone. Women's attitude is, 'What can you do for me?' It's me and not we!"

It's not that guys are assholes. It's that people are assholes. In relationships we can act selfishly—as arguably at times we should. But if we want to single out the biggest asshole, it's relationships themselves. Because the truth is, even if no one is acting irresponsibly, being in one still means you may get hurt. Dating means you may end up in the disappointing situation where you like someone more than he likes you. And breakups mean you're going to feel like crap, even if no one is at fault. But guy or girl, we face these realities and take these risks together.

The Asshole Myth Debunked, and What That Means for You

Hopefully by now you're thoroughly convinced that guys are emotional creatures who seek out companionship and connection. Not only do they want relationships (99% would want one with the "right girl"), for the majority, finding a relationship is a top priority (73% said finding a relationship was their primary interest in women). Guys care more about relationships than they care about sex (only 8% said they're interested in women primarily as people to have sex with). And when guys are in relationships, they fall in love deeply, prioritize their girlfriends, and are not "destined" to cheat. What all this means is that your dating strategies may need some adjusting. Here are three things to keep in mind:

1. IT'S OKAY TO WANT A RELATIONSHIP.

As girls, sometimes we're afraid to say we want relationships because we think it will push guys away. But a relationship is a perfectly okay thing to want. Guys want them too! Wanting a relationship with a guy isn't going to scare him off *unless* he doesn't want one with you. And if he doesn't want a relationship with you, it's because he doesn't like you, or doesn't like you enough, not because he's a guy and "guys hate relationships."

Hookups have their time and place. And there may be times when that's all you want and that's what feels good. But don't settle for a hookup arrangement if what you really want to be is a guy's girlfriend. Hooking up with him does not bring you any closer to being his girlfriend than not hooking up with him does. It only gives you a temporary fix, the immediate gratification of being with him, but in the end you'll just be left wanting more and feeling unfulfilled. '

Having strong feelings for a guy can seriously cloud your judgment about what situations are and aren't okay for you to be involved in. You may have to dig deep and be painfully honest with yourself in order to figure out if you're truly okay having a casual relationship with a guy you're really into. But do take the time to really analyze how you're feeling and get in touch with your true desires. When you don't, you set yourself up for heartbreak.

2. IT'S NOT OKAY TO USE SEX
AS A BARGAINING CHIP.

Because guys aren't actually controlled by sex, you can't use sex as a way to control them. All arguments about the morality of this aside, it just doesn't work. Hooking up with a guy is not going to make him like you. Sex is not bait that you can use to get a guy to fall for you. Maybe that works in melodramatic movies, but not in real life.

Will trying to lure a guy with the promise of sex get him? If he's really drunk, maybe it will get his penis for the night. But is that really what you're after? If you like a guy, impress him by asking him out, having fun with him, and showing him how down-to-earth, intelligent, and awesome you are.

The fact that a guy can't be manipulated through sex also means that *not* having sex with him isn't the secret to making him fall in love with you either. Guys are interested in girls for who they are, not just what their vaginas do (or, in this case, don't do). If a guy doesn't like you, he doesn't like you. And there is no formula for sleeping with him or not that is going to change his feelings.

3. YOU DON'T HAVE TO BE OVERLY SKEPTICAL.

Guys, on the whole, are not untrustworthy, and they are not destined to cheat. This means that if you have a boyfriend, don't freak every time he goes out with his friends. Being overly suspicious will only drive you crazy and push him away. Either you trust a guy or you don't. If you don't, and have reason to believe he's a sketchball, break up with him. But if you're skeptical just because he is a guy, you have to let it go. You can't try to control what he does; you just have to have faith that you trust him for a reason, and that if faced with temptation he's going to make responsible choices—just like you do.

If there is one time you *should* be overly skeptical of a guy's motives, it's if he's a guy you've just met at a bar. Many guys excused their sketchy sexual behavior with "We met in a bar, what does she expect?" They assumed that a girl in this situation "knows what she's getting herself into." If you meet a guy at a bar and sleep with him that night, know that more than likely you're getting yourself into a one-night stand. If that's your goal, fine. But if you're taking some guy home expecting a relationship to flourish, think again. Sure, it might. But if a relationship is what you're looking for, that's probably not the best way to go about it. If you meet a guy at a bar and want to date him, get his number and meet up with him another night.

Are You Dating an Asshole?

We can spend so much time overanalyzing our relationships: the good, the bad, the ups, the downs. Why didn't he call? What is he thinking? When is he going to start acting more interested? But here's a basic question we often miss: Are you happy? Or are you sad? Both when you're with him and when you're not with him, do you feel good? Or do you feel insecure and uneasy?

The best advice I got following my breakup was this: "Everybody deserves to be in a relationship with someone they adore, and they deserve to feel adored by the someone they are with." There it is. The bottom line, the make-it-or-break-it ultimate question. As complex and varied as all relationships are, this is just so simple. Do you feel adored? Do you feel valued? Does the person make you feel happy and good about yourself? If the answers to those questions aren't a resounding yes, you are involved with an asshole.

And here's the real kicker: the guy himself may not actually be a jerk. But if what he's doing is hurting you, what's the difference? He may as well be some douchebag you met at a bar, because the end result is the same.

There may be 8 million things you hope to find in a guy. And maybe the guy you're with has 7 million of them. But making you feel good is a prerequisite. And if he's falling short there, it's not okay. I don't care how good-looking he is, how smart he is, how much fun you have with him, how dedicated he is to starving kids in Kenya, or if he's single-handedly curing cancer. If he doesn't make you feel good, he is not a good guy for you. Period. It's that simple.

Knowing the Difference Between a True Asshole and One Who's Just Playing the Part

Because so many guys are convinced that being "too nice" will make you lose interest, it's important to be able to distinguish an impostor asshole from a real one. An impostor asshole is a guy who plays it cool and acts like he's not blown away by you even when he is. He doesn't return your calls right away (though returns them eventually), sends you some short text messages, gives you "two compliments and one 'neg'" (a playful insult), and acts only mildly interested. Basically, if you've just started dating a guy who's actively trying to see you but acting a bit aloof, that's an impostor asshole.

A *real* asshole is a guy who doesn't want to do anything with you that doesn't take place in his bed or on his couch, even though you want something more. He's a guy who only calls you when he's drunk. He's the guy you're really into, have been seeing for months, but won't let the relationship progress or won't fully commit. The insight that one 26-year-old had on these types of situations sums it up pretty succinctly: "Guys are jerks 'cause they don't like you. If they did, they wouldn't be." If you're involved with a guy who doesn't like you, he's an asshole, and it's time to move on.

What if it's unclear? Some days it seems like he may just be playing it cool, and other days it seems like he doesn't care about you at all? In my experience, if you think you might be getting screwed over, you probably are. One guy offered this advice: "Girls need to start taking guys for who they are, and not what they want them to be. If there's smoke, there's fire; don't give him the benefit of the doubt."

If something in your gut is telling you to worry, it's telling you that for a reason. And it's not because you're "being crazy" or "being a girl." If a guy is giving you reasons to overanalyze, don't start making excuses that would make his behavior "okay"; take his actions at face value. If he were acting normal, or how you'd expect him to, you wouldn't be freaking out.

Of course, the best way to figure out a guy's feelings is simply to ask him. As one guy put it: "I think in most cases where some-one is a jerk, it comes down to poor communication, bad listen-ing, and misaligned expectations." Most men are not callous. At the end of the day, they don't want to hurt you. Will they plow through minor inklings and little signs that you are getting hurt? Possibly. But if you ask a guy point-blank how he feels and what he wants, he'll likely be honest with you. And after learning his feelings, you can then decide if it's a good idea to continue seeing him or not.

Getting an Asshole to Change His Tune

If you're dating a guy who treats you badly, your *only* move is to demand he treat you better and walk away. No guy will ever fall in love with a girl he doesn't respect. And if you let him walk on you and treat you like crap, he's not going to respect you. Your only option is to take control by ending it. Tell him, "I'm not going to put up with you treating me like this. If you fix A, B, and C, then I will think about dating you. But if that's not going to happen, forget about it."

Then, you walk away. If he does nothing, it's because he never cared about you in the first place and in that case the relationship was doomed from the start. If he was on the fence, seeing you stand up for yourself is going to make him respect you more and take the relationship more seriously. If he decides he wants to pursue something with you, he will come back and do it right. And here's the important part: He gets exactly one chance to do it right. If he acts better at first, only to go back to his old sketchball routine, forget it—it's over. For good this time.

There's a saying, "Men love bitches, and women love assholes." That's not true. What is true is that people are attracted to other self-sufficient people who stand up for themselves. A guy I met in Santa Monica told me: "You need to know a woman is competent and can get what she wants. You need to know that she's a fully functioning person by herself and that with you or without you she'd be okay."

No guy is going to like you more for not demanding anything from him, and letting him do whatever he wants. People want boundaries, and they want to be challenged. In all of the things that guys listed as being important traits they look for in a girlfriend, not a single one wrote anything to the effect of "she lets me do whatever I want."

It's not like a guy doesn't know when he's treating you badly. And when he is, he wants you to call him on it and say, "You're not going to treat me well? Fine. I don't need you, I'll go find another guy who's better." It takes two people to have a relationship. If one is a complete pushover, then the relationship is one person and one blow-up doll. And that's not a relationship. You can't be afraid to stand up for yourself, and if a guy is continually treating you badly, you can't be afraid to walk away.

Getting Away from an Asshole

Guys can be jerks. We can't control that. What we can control is what we do about it. No one is holding a gun to your head, keeping you in a relationship that makes you feel like crap. You can blame a guy up to a point, but you're only stuck dating an asshole when you're unwilling to do anything about it.

If a guy makes you feel bad, cut him out of your life. If he's your boyfriend, break up with him. If he's your partially-ex-a-little-bit-current-not-really-clear-what-he-is thing, stop sleeping with him. If he's that hookup you have feelings for who isn't showing interest in return, put an end to it.

Breakups suck. I get it. But you can't let the fear of a breakup keep you in a bad relationship. I'll walk you through it right now: You're going to cry, a lot. The first week you're going to lose your appetite, and the week after that you're going to want to eat everything sweet, salty, or greasy that you can imagine. You're going to get drunk on a Wednesday because that's close enough to Thursday and that almost counts as a weekend. You're going to spend hours on the phone with your friends. You may also spend hours on the phone with your relatives. You're going to realize how much love and affection you have in your life separate from anything you're getting (or not getting, as the case may be) from a guy.

Slowly, you're going to move on. Eventually, you're going to get over it. And finally, you will meet someone else. See? That wasn't so bad.

One of the hardest things about ending it may be all the questions left unanswered. Why wasn't he into it? Why was he into it and then changed his mind? You may never know. But not having complete closure doesn't mean you can't decide to close it. It's never worth staying involved with someone (physically or emotionally) simply in hopes of figuring out why. Because the "why" is never as important as the "what," and that you already know: He didn't like you enough, or he wasn't making you happy.

Avoiding Assholes Once and for All

In a conversation with some guys in Houston, I asked: "If you started dating a girl and were pulling all the usual 'I don't really give a shit' stunts, and she told you to stop, would you? Like, if she made very clear that the asshole shtick didn't do it for her, would you cut the crap?"

"Well, yeah," one answered. "If a girl laid it down, I would change." But then, they all agreed that this would never happen, that a girl would never demand this, because girls like assholes. "Look, we'll fit the market. You created it; we'll fit it. Just tell us what you want."

Guys act macho and unemotional because that's how they think we want them to behave. They act like they're not that into us because they believe it's the only way that we'd be into them. If we want guys to conduct themselves differently, we have to tell them to—"create the market," so to speak. How do we do this? Three easy steps:

Step 1: When you meet a guy, be honest with yourself about what it is you want from him. Sometimes it may be just sex, sometimes it may be short-term companionship, and sometimes you may want a more serious relationship. Don't delude yourself about which one of those things it actually is that you want, because mixing them up doesn't work well no matter which way the wires are crossed. (Getting into a serious relationship with a guy you're actually only sexually attracted to doesn't turn out much better than settling for just sex with a guy you have real feelings for.)

Step 2: Once you know what it is that you want out of your relationship with a guy, make your intentions clear. Sometimes that will be through actions: passing on going home with a guy the night you meet him, but suggesting you meet up for a drink the next week. Other times you're going to have to spell it out: "You blowing me off and acting sketchy isn't going to work for me. I like you and would like to try having a real relationship. But I'm not going to be your sort-of girlfriend who you sometimes call."

Step 3: And this one is the most important: If your needs aren't being met, or a guy is treating you badly, get out of the relationship. Life is about making compromises. You can't get everything you want, and you have to learn to live with that. But being treated well by the guy you're involved with—*that* is a nonnegotiable.

. . .

Avoiding assholes is not impossible, though it will require staying actively committed to doing so. At times, it will be challenging. You may have to leave a guy you really like—or even love. But there are too many good guys out there to let yourself stay with one who's not treating you well. As one guy so wisely wrote: "The universe is vast; there *are* sensitive guys. I listen to Eminem and Norah Jones. There, I said it."

Dating is a daunting task. And meeting a guy you like, who likes you back, *and* who you're compatible with, can sometimes feel like an impossibility. But in the words of a 27-year-old: "The good news is, you only need one good one."

Washington, DC: Keeping the Faith

A book about guys, and I'm going to end it talking about my dad. Freud would have a field day.

The last stop on my journey was Washington, DC. My dad had a conference there, and we coordinated our trips to be at the same time. I'd go out and talk to guys, he'd look over his papers, and then we'd meet up in our downtime to go to a museum or eat dinner. I was only there two days, but I realize now it's the most time we've spent alone together in years. And as your parents get older, that one-on-one time you always think you can put off for later feels more meaningful when it actually happens.

At the end of the trip, my dad hugged me good-bye and tucked me into a cab with my backpack: "I put an apple and some M&M's in the front pocket, so if you get hungry on the train you'll have something to eat. You know"—he grabbed my shoulder for emphasis—"the brain is the most metabolically active organ in the body." Two things my dad loves to remind me whenever I'm working are that thinking burns a lot of calories, so I'd better eat a lot, and that "sleep is a weapon," so I'd better do a lot of that too.

He leaned in and kissed me on the cheek: "We're so proud of you, bub."

Eating the M&M's on the train ride home, it occurred to me: Here I've been chasing men around the country for months, trying to figure out if they sucked or not, and somehow I completely neglected to think about the man in my life whom I've known the longest. The one who would get me out of school early on my birthday to play basketball. The one who had the woman from the wine shop by my apartment pick up flowers for me when I finished a draft of my book. The one I was so mad at for disliking one of my boyfriends for seemingly no reason . . . until my mom told me, "He'll warm up, sweetie. It's just that in his eyes, no one will ever be good enough for you."

In a romantic context, we're so quick to jump on guys for being jerks. We're so willing to assume horrible things about them and write them off as incomplete human beings. We make generalizations that "all guys are this way" or "all guys will do that." But we forget that all the wonderful, nurturing men we know in a different context—they're guys too. The men who have helped us grow up, been there to support us through the bad times, and cheered us on during the good—they're still male. Our fathers, grandfathers, uncles, mentors, teachers, and coaches all have that same Y chromosome we're convinced makes the guys we date so bad.

Guys mature with age and that is part of it. But these guys that we date and get so discouraged by, they're going to grow up to be the next generation of doting fathers, uncles, and grand-fathers.

In order to get there, some may need slight nudges in the right direction. Others may need to hear exactly how badly what they did made you feel. Many just have some things they need to figure out for themselves. But they all need for us to believe in them. Believe that the men they are is not that entirely different from the men we know they can be.

I'm not sure whether it's worse that I started this section talking about my dad or that I'm ending it with a quote from *The Game*. But I found it especially poignant that this detailed document of male pickup artists included this thought: "Men are not dogs. We merely think we are and, on occasion, act as if we are.

But by believing in our nobler nature, women have the amazing power to inspire us to live up to it."

Guys aren't assholes. Just like girls aren't crazy. And even though we've been led to believe men and women are so fundamentally different and riddled with incompatibilities, that's just not true. It's time we call a truce—and stop blaming each other for the difficulties inherent in intimate relationships. We're all in this together, and relationships will get easier only when we learn to have more faith in each other.

1. Age: _____ Occupation: _____

2. What is your highest completed education?
   ___ Graduate school degree
   ___ College degree
   ___ Some college
   ___ High school graduate
   ___ Did not graduate from high school

3. What is your racial/ethnic background?
   ___ White
   ___ Hispanic
   ___ African American
   ___ Asian American
   ___ Native American
   ___ Other (please specify) _____

4. What is your relationship status?
   ___ Single
   ___ Hooking up with someone
   ___ Dating someone
   ___ Relationship
   ___ Serious relationship

5. How many days do you usually wait to contact a girl after a first date?

___ One day

___ Two days

___ Three days

___ About a week

___ More than a week

6. If a girl asks you out, is it a turn-on or too aggressive, or does it not matter to you either way?

___ Turn-on

___ Does not matter either way

___ Too aggressive

7. You got her number and then never called. Why?

_____

_____

8. What is your preferred method of talking to a girl you like?

___ Facebook

___ Texting

___ Calling

___ E-mailing

___ Other (specify) _____

9. You've been on a few dates with a girl/hooked up a few times. You always return her texts, but don't make any plans to actually see her. Why? _____

_____

_____

_____

10. Before a first date, how nervous are you on a scale from 1 (not scared) to 10 (shitting in your pants)?

    1   2   3   4   5   6   7   8   9   10

11. What things turn you off the most on a date? _____
    _____

12. The morning after a hookup, do you usually want the girl to leave right away?
    ___ Yes
    ___ No
    ___ Depends (explain) _____

13. You've been dating a girl for a while but haven't had the "you're my girlfriend" talk yet. Most likely, what is the reason?
    ___ It's an awkward conversation to have
    ___ You're not sure if she wants a commitment
    ___ You're not sure if you want to commit to her
    ___ Other (please specify) _____

14. You've lost interest in a girl you've been seeing—what are the signs?
    _____

15. Would you ever take a girl on a few dates, text her frequently, and fake an interest in her or her life (but not fake your willingness to have a relationship) just to get her in bed?
    ___ Yes
    ___ No

16. You've slept with a girl a few times but you are not dating. Do you have any feelings for her?
    ___ A lot
    ___ Some
    ___ A little
    ___ None at all

17. You didn't kiss a girl after your first date. Most likely it is because:
    ___ You didn't like her much
    ___ You wussed out
    ___ You didn't have the opportunity
    ___ You thought it might be too forward
    ___ Other (Please explain) _____

18. How important are the following traits in a girlfriend, on a scale of 1 (not important) to 5 (very important)?

Good looks	1	2	3	4	5
Nice/Caring	1	2	3	4	5
Sense of humor	1	2	3	4	5
Ambition	1	2	3	4	5
Intelligence	1	2	3	4	5

    Other very important traits (please specify) _____

19. Do you treat a girl differently from the beginning if you want a relationship with her?
    ___ No
    ___ Yes. If yes, how? _____

20. If a girl sleeps with you too soon, will it mess up the chances of a relationship?

___ No

___ Yes. If yes, why? _____

21. How soon is "too soon" to have sex? _____

22. You meet a girl and hook up with her that night—can that turn into a relationship?

___ No

___ Yes

___ Depends (explain)_____

23. Can a serial hookup relationship turn into a real relationship?

___ No

___ Yes

24. Would you lie about the degree of commitment you're willing to offer a girl in order to sleep with her?

___ No

___ Yes

25. Would most guys lie about the degree of commitment they're willing to offer a girl in order to sleep with her?

___ No

___ Yes

26. Your primary interest in women is (choose one):

___ Someone to have sex with

___ Someone to potentially have a relationship with

___ Someone for companionship/short-term dating

___ Someone to impress your friends

27. Do you feel a sense of responsibility for the emotional well-being of the girls you're romantically involved with?
    __ Very much
    __ Somewhat
    __ A little
    __ Not at all

28. Do you feel a sense of responsibility for the emotional well-being of the girls you've had sex with?
    __ Very much
    __ Somewhat
    __ A little
    __ Not at all

29. If you found the right girl, would you want to be in a relationship?
    __ No
    __ Yes

30. Who cheats more, guys or girls?
    __ Guys
    __ Girls
    __ Both the same

31. Would you cheat on your girlfriend if you thought she'd never find out?
    __ No
    __ Yes

32. If you had engaged in the following activities with a girl who isn't your girlfriend, would you consider it cheating? Circle yes or no for each.

    Kissing: No   Yes

    Emotional affair (excessive e-mailing, calls, texts, etc., but nothing physical):   No   Yes

    Cuddling while sleeping in the same bed: No   Yes

    Oral sex: No   Yes

    Intercourse: No   Yes

33. You and your girlfriend have been seriously dating for a while, you both have deep feelings for each other, but you haven't said, "I love you." Do you love her? And if so, why haven't you told her? If not, what is the difference between the feelings you have for her and love?

    _____

    _____

    _____

34. Ideally, would you want to get married someday?

    __ No

    __ Yes. If yes, at what age? _____

35. Who comes first: your girlfriend or the guys?

    __ Girlfriend all the way

    __ Girlfriend, by a hair

    __ It's a tie

    __ Guys, by a hair

    __ Guys all the way

36. What about your girlfriend or your relationship makes you
    question your relationship the most? _____
    _____
    _____

37. Is there anything significant you're hiding from your girlfriend or
    lying to her about?
    ___ No
    ___ Yes. If yes, specify _____

38. When/if you have a girlfriend, do you still watch porn?
    ___ No (please explain) _____
    ___ Yes (please explain) _____

39. Romantically speaking, on the whole, do guys act like jerks
    to girls?
    ___ No
    ___ Yes

40. Romantically speaking, on the whole, do you act like a jerk
    to girls?
    ___ No
    ___ Yes

Feel free to add any other thoughts you might have:
_____
_____
_____
_____
_____

APPENDIX 2:
ONLINE SURVEY

I posted the link to this survey on the pages of the most random male Facebook friends I had and asked them to take it and pass it on to their friends. (After this a friend advised me: "You know, maybe these poor guys don't want a link to a sex survey on their Facebook walls." Whoops.) I also sent the link to every guy in my e-mail contacts and asked that they pass it on to friends from high school, college, work, and any other straight, unmarried, 22-to-45-year-old guys they knew. In total, 200 guys filled out this follow-up survey.

Instructions

This is a survey for guys ages 22 to 45 who date women and are not married or engaged. If you do not fit these criteria, please do not fill out.

Please be as honest as possible, and know that your answers are completely confidential and anonymous. If there is a question that does not apply to you, please leave it blank. As you read through the questions, choose the answer that BEST reflects your feelings.

Thanks so much for your time!

1. How old are you? _____

2. What is your highest completed education?
   ___ Graduate school
   ___ College degree
   ___ Some college
   ___ High school graduate
   ___ Did not graduate from high school

3. If you sleep with a girl "too soon" (whenever that may be in your opinion), what are the chances it will mess up the possibility of a serious relationship?
   ___ No chance at all for a relationship.
   ___ A small chance for a relationship.
   ___ Some chance of a relationship.
   ___ When you sleep with a girl has absolutely no bearing on whether or not you end up in a relationship with her.

4. If you meet a girl and hook up with her that night (but don't have sex), what are the chances that will turn into a serious relationship?
   ___ Impossible, I wouldn't date a girl I hooked up with right away.
   ___ Unlikely, but if I really liked her it could happen.
   ___ It's possible, though I might be hesitant because we hooked up right away.
   ___ Hooking up with her makes no difference one way or the other in regard to whether or not we get involved.
   ___ None of these even remotely describes my feelings on the issue.

5. If you meet a girl and sleep with her that night, what are the chances that will turn into a serious relationship?
___ Impossible, I wouldn't date a girl I slept with right away.
___ Unlikely, but if I really liked her it could happen.
___ It's possible, though I might be hesitant because we slept together right away.
___ Sleeping with her right away makes no difference one way or the other in regard to whether or not we get involved.
___ None of these even remotely describes my feelings on the issue.

6. If you have a friends-with-benefits/hookup relationship with a girl, what are the chances that will turn into a serious relationship?
___ No chance at all.
___ A small chance, but not very likely.
___ Fifty-fifty either way.
___ It's very likely feelings will develop over time.

7. How do you feel when a girl gives you instructions—in a nice way—for what to do in bed? (Assuming this is a girl you care about.)
___ Awesome. A girl knowing what she likes is hot.
___ I'm happy to be getting instructions on what to do.
___ Mixed feelings. I'm happy to know, but it's awkward at the time.
___ Mixed feelings. I'm happy to know, but it's also kind of offensive.
___ I'd rather she keep her feelings to herself.

8. How do you feel about going down on a girl? (Choose any that apply.)

___ It's a turn-on.

___ It's gross.

___ I like to do it but wish she'd tell me what to do down there.

___ I try to avoid it.

___ I like to do it, but many girls don't want me to.

___ No strong feelings about it one way or another.

___ I like it because it makes her feel good.

9. You've been on a few dates with a girl you like. Do you want her to be contacting you in between dates? (Check all that apply.)

___ Yes, it's nice to hear from a girl you like.

___ Only via text, no calls.

___ Mostly text, occasional phone calls.

___ As long as it's not excessive (excessive being every day).

___ As long as it's not excessive (excessive being multiple times a day).

___ As long as it's not excessive (excessive being texting me before I've responded, and after I've responded with short answers showing I can't talk).

___ I prefer to always be the one initiating contact.

10. You've been on a few dates with a girl you like. How often do you expect to see her?

___ Once a week

___ 1 or 2 times per week, depending on the week

___ 2 or 3 times per week, depending on the week

___ 3 or 4 times per week, depending on the week

___ More than 4 times per week

11. Would you cheat on a girl you were in love with and thought might be "the one"?
    ___ No
    ___ Yes

12. If you are dating a girl with the intention of possibly pursuing a relationship, at what point can you have sex with her without it negatively affecting your feelings about her?
    ___ First date
    ___ 2 dates
    ___ 3 dates
    ___ 4 or 5 dates
    ___ Once I know her well.
    ___ Once we love each other.
    ___ Once we get married.
    ___ When I have sex with a girl I'm dating would never negatively affect my feelings about her.

What percentage of guys are true assholes? Using eight questions from the original survey, I assigned positive asshole points for questions guys answered like a jerk, and negative asshole points for questions they answered like a great guy. A neutral answer got zero points. (For example, guys didn't get a negative asshole point for saying they wouldn't cheat, since not cheating should be expected behavior, not above and beyond the call of boyfriend duty.) These are the questions I used, and the point values assigned to each answer. Like golf, the lower the score the better:

Question 12: The morning after a hookup do you usually want the girl to leave right away?

Yes = +1
Depends = 0
No = −1

Question 15: Would you ever take a girl on a few dates, text her frequently, and fake an interest in her or her life (but not fake your willingness to have a relationship) just to get her in bed?

Yes = +1
No = 0

Question 24: Would you lie about your relationship intentions in order to sleep with a girl?

    Yes = +1

    No = 0

Question 27: Do you feel a sense of responsibility for the emotional well-being of the girls you're romantically involved with?

    "A little" or "Not at all" = +1

    "Somewhat" = 0

    "Very Much" = −1

Question 28: Do you feel a sense of responsibility for the emotional well-being of the girls you've had sex with?

    "A little" or "Not at all" = +1

    "Somewhat" = 0

    "Very Much" = −1

Question 31: Would you cheat on your girlfriend if you thought she'd never find out?

    Yes = +1

    No = 0

Question 35: Who comes first: your girlfriend or the guys?

    "Guys, by a hair" or "Guys all the way"= +1

    "It's a tie" = 0

    "Girlfriend, by a hair" or "Girlfriend all the way" = −1

Question 40: Romantically speaking, on the whole, do you act like a jerk to girls?

    Yes = +1

    No = 0

The best a guy could do was score a –4. The worst a guy could do was score an 8. The 21% of guys who scored between –2 and –4, are the ones I labeled "saints." The 31% of guys who scored either a –1 or a 0, I labeled "good guys." The 12% who scored a 1, I called "human." The 20% who scored a 2 or 3, I called "misguided." And finally, the 16% who scored a 4 or higher were the ones I considered to be "true assholes."

ACKNOWLEDGMENTS

This book would not exist if it weren't for my editor, Gabrielle Moss, who adopted it when it was just a 20-page proposal, and both shared and shaped my vision for what it could become. Gaby, I cannot thank you enough for all of your support throughout every step of this process.

To all you men (who don't want to be named by name) who took the time to call and e-mail me regularly about your love lives, I am so grateful you let me share your experiences, and you will all be in my thoughts moving forward, even if your thoughts are no longer in my notebooks. To the many guys who filled out the survey in person and online, thanks for your "five minutes" (that was actually more like 20). To the guys who took the time to discuss these issues with me in depth, thank you for digging deep, examining your feelings, and giving me a better understanding.

To the statistician (my mom) who took all of these numbers and helped me understand them and turn them into something meaningful, thanks for making your day job your night and weekend job as well.

Many thanks to all the friends and family who helped me while traveling, whether it was sneaking into their office to print out 500 copies of the survey, spending hours collating and stapling, giving me a place to sleep, or actually hitting the streets with me to harass men: Robert and Louisa Paushter, Elizabeth Kirkhart, Lucia Di Poi, Meghan Gambling, Abbey Lichten, Ali Montgomery, and Becca Halperin. And finally, a bottomless thank you to the people in my life who continue to support me both personally and professionally: Robin Straus, Jodi Solomon, Todd Lichten, Corin Lines, Noffar Bar, Leah Oster-Katz, Anna Corliss, Sari David, Sarah Wilburn, Erin Allweiss, Melissa Crossley, Melinda Rhodebeck, Nikias Stefanakis, and finally my parents, Roger and Jane Madison.

NOTES

How I Became an Assholologist

1. Landau, Elizabeth. "Men Have Upper Hand in Sexual Economy." The Chart-CNN.com Blogs. 18 January 2011. Web. 22 April 2011. <http://thechart.blogs.cnn.com/2011/01/18/men-have-upper-hand-in-sexual-economy/>.
2. Dush, C.M.K., and P. R. Amato. "Consequences of Relationship Status and Quality for Subjective Well-being." *Journal of Social and Personal Relationships.* 22 (2005): 607–627.
3. Hatfield, E., and S. Sprecher. "Measuring Passionate Love in Intimate Relationships." *Journal of Adolescence.* 9 (1986): 383–410.
4. Rotermann, M. "Marital Breakdown and Subsequent Depression." *Health Report.* 18.2 (2007): 33–44.
5. Pedersen, W. C., et al. "Evolved Sex Differences in the Number of Partners Desired? The Long and Short of It." *Psychological Science.* 13 (2002): 157–161.
6. Levant, Ronald F., Ed.D., MBA, ABPP. Personal Interview. 15 April 2010.
7. Ibid.
8. Hyde, J. S. "New Directions in the Study of Gender Similarities and Differences." *Current Directions in Psychological Science.* 16 (2007): 259–263.

"A Fake Reputation Is All a Man Has"

1. Levant, Ronald F., Ed.D., MBA, ABPP. Personal Interview. 15 April 2010.
2. Kiecolt-Glaser, J. K., and T. L. Newton. "Marriage and Health: His and Hers." *Psychological Bulletin.* 127 (2001): 472–503.

3. Eberhart, N. K., and C. L. Hammen. "Interpersonal Predictors of Onset of Depression During the Transition to Adulthood." *Personal Relationships.* 13 (2006): 195–206.

4. Lillard, L. L., and W. A. Panis. "Marital Status and Mortality: The Role of Health." *Demography.* 33 (1996): 313–327.

5. Dush, C.M.K., and P. R. Amato. "Consequences of Relationship Status and Quality for Subjective Well-being." *Journal of Social and Personal Relationships.* 22 (2005): 607–627.

6. Hyde, J. S. "New Directions in the Study of Gender Similarities and Differences." *Current Directions in Psychological Science.* 16 (2007): 259–263.

7. Ibid.

8. Eliot, Lise. *Pink Brain, Blue Brain: How Small Differences Grow into Troublesome Gaps—And What We Can Do About It.* New York: Houghton Mifflin Harcourt, 2009.

9. Kuhn, Cynthia, Ph.D. Personal Interview. 23 April 2010.

10. Ibid.

11. Allen, D. "Condoms: From Inception to Now." *Journal of the Health Resource Center.* 5.2 (2006): 25–30.

12. Pedersen, W. C., et al. "Evolved Sex Differences in the Number of Partners Desired? The Long and Short of It." *Psychological Science.* 13 (2002): 157–161.

13. Miller, L. C., and S. A. Fishkin. "On the Dynamics of Human Bonding and Reproductive Success: Seeking 'Windows' on the 'Adapted-for' Human-Environmental Interface." In J. A. Simpson and D. T. Kenrick (eds.) *Evolutionary Social Psychology.* Mahwah, NJ: Erlbaum, 1997.

14. Cervantes, C. A., and M. A. Callanan. "Labels and Explanations in Mother-Child Emotion Talk: Age and Gender Differentiation." *Developmental Psychology.* 34 (1998): 88–98.

15. Evans, L., and K. Davies. "No Sissy Boys Here: A Content Analysis of the Representation of Masculinity in Elementary School Reading Textbooks." *Sex Roles.* 42 (2000): 255–270.

16. Levant, Ronald F., Ed.D., MBA, ABPP. Personal Interview. 15 April 2010.

17. Cochran, Sam V. Ph.D. Personal Interview. 14 April 2010.

18. Levant, Ronald F., Ed.D., MBA, ABPP. Personal Interview. 15 April 2010.

Does He Not Care Like I Do?

1. Simon, R. W., and A. E. Barrett. "Nonmarital Romantic Relationships and Mental Health in Early Adulthood." *Journal of Health and Social Behavior.* 51 (2010): 168–182.

2. Levant, Ronald F., Ed.D., MBA, ABPP. Personal Interview. 15 April 2010.

3. Bretherton, I. et al. "Learning to Talk About Emotions: A Functionalist Perspective." *Child Development.* 57 (1986): 529–548.

4. Brody, L. R. "The Socialization of Gender Differences in Emotional Expression: Display Rules, Infant Temperament, and Differentiation." In A. Fischer (ed.), *Gender and Emotion.* Cambridge, UK: Cambridge University Press, 2000.

5. Brody, L. R. "Gender, Emotional Expression, and Parent-Child Boundaries." In R. Kavanaugh, et al. (eds.) *Human Feelings: Explorations in Affect Development and Meaning.* Mahwah, NJ: Erlbaum, 1996.

6. Fivush, R., et al. "Gender Differences in Parent-Child Emotion Narratives." *Sex Roles.* 42 (2000): 233–253.

7. Adler, N. E., et al. "Psychological Factors in Abortion." *American Psychologist.* 47 (1992): 1194–1204.

8. Kring, A. M., and A. H. Gordon. "Sex Differences in Emotion: Expression, Experience, and Physiology." *Journal of Personality and Social Psychology.* 74 (1998): 686–703.

9. Canary, D. J., and T. M. Emmers-Sommer. *Sex and Gender Differences in Personal Relationships.* New York: Guilford Press, 1997.

10. Lillard, L. L., and W. A. Panis. "Marital Status and Mortality: The Role of Health." *Demography.* 33 (1996): 313–327.

11. Plagnol, Anke C., and Richard A. Easterlin. "Aspirations, Attainments, and Satisfaction: Life Cycle Differences Between American Women and Men." *Journal of Happiness Studies.* 9 (2008): 601–619.

12. Kreider, R. M. "Number, Timing, and Duration of Marriages and Divorces: 2001: Current Population Reports." US Dept of Commerce, US Census Bureau. (2005): 1–17.

13. Heiman, J. R. "The Physiology of Erotica: Women's Sexual Arousal." *Psychology Today.* 8 (1975): 90–94.

Is His Sexuality More Complex
Than "Pork It"?

1. Petersen, J., and J. Hyde. "A Meta-Analytic Review of Research on Gender Differences in Sexuality, 1993–2007." *Psychological Bulletin*. 136 (2010): 21–38.

2. Alexander, M. G., and T. D. Fisher. "Truth and Consequences: Using the Bogus Pipeline to Examine Sex Differences in Self-Reported Sexuality." *Journal of Sex Research*. 40 (2003): 27–35.

3. Atwood, J. D., and L. Schwartz. "Cyber-Sex: The New Affair Treatment Considerations." *Journal of Couple and Relationship Therapy*. 1 (2002): 37–56.

Good Thinking, Asshole!

1. Kaplan, H. S., and C. J. Sager. "Sexual Patterns at Different Ages." *Medical Aspects of Human Sexuality*. 5 (1971): 10–23.

2. Ibid.

INDEX